Cultural Capita

Teacher led research on the impact of arts and cultural education

Edited by Anita Kerwin-Nye & Franziska Florack

notdeadfish publishing

First published in the UK in October 2016 by NotDeadFish Publishing
Website: www.notdeadfish.co.uk
Contact: matt@notdeadfish.co.uk
Produced by A New Direction & NotDeadFish

A.N.D A new direction for arts, culture and young london

notdeadfish

All rights reserved
© NotDeadFish Publishing
ISBN 978-0-9955641-0-7

Table of Contents

INTRODUCTION TO THE CULTURAL LEADERS PROGRAMME	1
THE RESEARCH PROJECTS	5
INCREASING PARTICIPATION IN THE ARTS	16
Corelli College – City Year, Art and the National Gallery	16
Kings Avenue School – Our school band	25
Hamstead School – Through the looking glass – and what we found there	31
WORKING CROSS-CURRICULAR	41
Bishop Ramsey – A cross-curricular project between Expressive Arts and RE	41
Hampstead School – The Concrete Garden	49
ACTION RESEARCH AS PROFESSIONAL DEVELOPMENT	61
Mayflower Primary School – The use of visual arts to increase children's confidence in spoken language and discussions	61
Greenvale School – Action research on the impact of music workshops for students with complex needs	67
QEII Jubilee School – How can Creative Arts support the engagement of hard to reach young people?	76
ARTS AWARD AND ITS IMPACT	84
Lansbury Lawrence Community School – Can art help children raise attainment in reading?	84
Chingford Academies Trust – Encouraging participation, learning and achievement in the arts through interaction with Arts Award, working with young people in receipt of Pupil Premium funding	90
Queensbridge Primary School – The impact of introducing the Discover Arts Award to Pupil Premium Children in Year 2	102

Introduction to the Cultural Leaders programme

Cultural Leaders is a partnership between A New Direction and NotDeadFish. Over 2015/16 we worked with 24 senior teachers of the arts from across London schools to create a powerful new community of advocates for cultural education as an entitlement for all young people.

London has secured a world reputation as a cultural powerhouse. Seven out of ten visitors to London say culture is the reason they chose to come to the city. But, despite this global position, not all London's young people benefit from access to culture.

There are huge inequalities affecting young Londoners' cultural engagement:

- Two in five of children from the poorest homes are read to every day compared to nearly four in five of those from the richest families.
- Pupils qualifying for Free School Meals are less likely to take part in all forms of arts activity and 12% less likely to take part in an after-school club than their peers.

Young people from lower income families are far more likely to have their first experience of the arts through school rather than at home (46%–30% respectively).

Schools are a key route to a cultural entitlement for all but arts leaders in schools report an increasing sense of isolation.

Cultural Leaders provided our participants with the chance to connect with other arts and cultural professionals at five conferences. These afternoon-long meetings included guest lectures, networking time and opportunities to discuss the Cultural Leaders' own action research projects. Some of the sessions took place at the Museum of London and others at the Tate Modern, taking advantage of the unique creative atmosphere of those spaces.

Any middle or senior leader with a passion for the arts was welcome to apply for the programme, which was funded by AND. Schools were only asked to contribute the cover for the conferences and some research time. Most importantly, they had to be committed to AND's vision for half of London's schools to join the Arts Mark programme and to make a real difference to the arts and cultural education of the capital and beyond.

The Cultural Leaders programme focused on four key areas:

- An exploration of what works in cultural education, drawing on the best practice of participant schools and input from cultural education providers.
- Gaining an understanding of cultural education in the context of wider school improvement and curriculum development, including through input from Ofsted, exam boards and school improvement leaders.
- Developing the skills to advocate for and be a leader of cultural education including media training, building coaching skills, learning about programme development and fundraising and opportunities to present at conferences and write articles for publication.
- Action Research skills: Participants were asked to identify one area of cultural education provision that they wanted to improve over the duration of the project around which they – working with colleagues across the programme – could develop an action learning project to implement.

The five conferences covered the importance of Artsmark and Action Research, using research to raise attention and funding, collaborating with others, raising attainment in schools and inspirational practice. With the aim of developing the skills of the cultural leaders to connect schools and to share 'what works' across the London system the programme had inputs across communications and social media; models of leadership and school to school support; project development and fundraising and research.

Cultural leaders were supported to take on a system leadership role; speaking at events; supporting their neighbouring schools and inputting into policy and practice.

As part of their work – and recognising the power of teacher led research both as a tool for continuing professional development and as a route for sharing effective practice – the cohort were encouraged to identify an issue around access to cultural education that they wanted to address and were supported to develop a short intervention.

This book captures the learning from eleven of the cultural leaders' research projects. It both celebrates the fantastic work that arts teachers do in school every day and highlights areas for potential additional investment and research as we move towards an increasing focus on a school led system.

Thanks to all of the cultural leaders who gave up time both to attend the five conference sessions and also to work on a research project that meant additional time on top of a busy school day. Thanks also to the schools who provided release time and the many cultural, education and third sector organisations that provided input into the programme.

The cultural leaders' generosity in sharing their learning illustrates their commitment to improving outcomes for all of London's children and young people. Their work over the last year has reached over 1600 school leaders, parents and governors to advocate for the importance of a cultural education for all and their ongoing commitment leaves us feeling the future of cultural education in London is in good hands.

A New Direction

A New Direction is a charity that helps London create, think and learn. They work in partnership to create positive change across schools, education and communities to ensure that all children and young people get the most out of London's extraordinary creative and cultural offer.

A New Direction want London to be a city where:

- cultural education is the best in the world
- young people are able to access and influence culture
- the right platforms are in place to identify and nourish young people's creative talents.

This is the right of all young Londoners – regardless of wealth, geography or luck.

www.anewdirection.org.uk

NotDeadFish

NotDeadFish is a social enterprise committed to improving collaboration between charities and schools; supporting organisations with the best services and boosting individuals with the best ideas.

We believe that outcomes for children and young people improve when organisations work together.

Our work focuses on finding charities, schools and other not for profits that have effective solutions to support children and young people and help them to create the best strategy to sustain and scale their work.

www.notdeadfish.co.uk

The research projects

Over the six months of the Cultural Leaders scheme, all participants engaged in a research project of their own choosing. This project saw them implement or increase a cultural provision in their school. As the provision took place (and at the end of it) Cultural Leaders measured whether the project had an impact on the members of their school.

In professional terms their investigations were 'action research projects'. This means that they were responsible for arranging their 'intervention' (the cultural provision) as well as the research. This type of research comes with a lot of power as the researcher is solely responsible for the design of their study, but it also bears its own limitations as there is only a limited review process.

One of the skills the project tried to pass on to the Cultural Leaders was to take the stance of a positive but critical research designer. While some Cultural Leaders had previously engaged in research through their PGCEs or degrees, many found the process of thinking through both the intervention and the research a challenge. NotDeadFish helped by providing regular feedback both online and in person. We also issued the Cultural Leaders with a 'Beginners Guide to Research'.

There were three stages to the research. Although these theoretically took place in order, Cultural Leaders had to consider all three at the start of the scheme. A new cultural provision (their 'intervention') could not be planned fully without thinking about what kind of impact they would like to measure and how they were going to use the data they would gather.

As the projects went on, the Cultural Leaders started to share experiences and potential pitfalls with each other. A real sense of camaraderie developed and on more than one occasion the 'Research First Aid' part of the Cultural Leaders session led to stimulating and interesting debates. Teachers realised that Action Research takes time but also praised the useful insights they were provided with through their work.

All Cultural Leaders were asked to complete questionnaires during the on the usefulness of the programme which charted their self-assessed progress in seven areas. While they already felt extremely confident on topics such as 'understanding of how a broad range of cultural education supports the curriculum' and others, there was slightly less confidence with regards to 'knowledge and understanding of current debates and research on effective pedagogy in cultural education', showing a potential divide between skills which help with resources and those which enable them to assess the work they have done with students.

At the end of the project, Cultural Leaders felt that they had improved in all aspects, however understanding research on pedagogies was the most increased area. Where teachers had rated themselves 2.7 out of 5 before, they saw a 50% increase in skill, now assessing themselves as a level 4. Generally, teachers also said that being part of the scheme had enabled them to engage with wider audiences and schools in partnerships and networks. Overall, Cultural Leaders reached out to a staggering 1624 education and cultural professionals, parents and governors!

While participants felt that their research skills had improved over the course of the project, many acknowledged that it had been a challenging journey. Time to undertake an extra research project was difficult to come by and at least two Cultural Leaders requested and were granted additional time by their senior management teams to complete their action research. This support from the senior management teams is encouraging: action research is important to both teachers and schools.

Summarising the benefits of the programme, Cultural Leaders reported a large increase in self-confidence and resourcefulness; a new ability to raise funds for further cultural projects was praised by many.

As the Cultural Leader projects developed, four topics naturally emerged:

- Increasing participation in the arts
- Cross-curricular collaboration
- Action research as professional development
- Arts Award and its impact.

While each Cultural Leader journey was unique, the participants of these individual groups had similar values and research foci: their stories complement each other and are a testament to the diversity which can be reached even within one area of research.

Our first group of projects centres around increased participation in the arts. The three Cultural Leaders who authored this section focused on a change in culture as well as practice: How can we make the arts more attractive to our students, resulting in higher participation? And what do arts projects give to students who engage with them? Creativity, and a real desire to understand the benefits of arts practice are at the heart of this section.

Shermaine planned an arts project in collaboration with City Year, a group of young adults who encourage students' love of learning. Working with City Year and the National Gallery, she wanted to give her students the opportunity to connect with paintings they would normally not have access to. Shermaine's Year 7 students showed a lack of confidence and low academic achievement but an aptitude for art: encouraging them to get involved in analysis and all kinds of visual arts encouraged them to come out of their shell and learn from the positive role models of City Year. At the end of the project, students felt more confident and felt that art had enabled them to access new skills, such as teamwork and pride in their own work.

Shermaine found that it was particularly challenging to work and research with an ever changing cohort of students: during her project many of the young research participants left or joined the school, making comparative questionnaires very difficult. This is a view echoed in many of the following reports and worth paying special attention to. Not only did the Cultural Leaders engage in their research projects in addition to their everyday responsibilities in the schools, but they were also researching in an environment which is not always the most accommodating in terms of comparative data. Educational settings are notoriously changeable and teachers have to be creative to plan action research projects which will stand the test of critical analysis.

Savi increased the provision of the arts in her school by encouraging the formation of a school band. She had felt that many of the musically gifted and talented children at the school needed further opportunities to hone their skills and shine to the best of their ability. Although she tried to engage children of all primary school ages, the final band only included committed students from Year 5 and Year 6, which in itself provided an interesting learning journey. As the project progressed, members of the band improved their understanding of musical language as well as teamwork and playing skills.

A large part of Savi's project celebrated the students' own proactive wish to keep the band going and work towards the final performances. The children chose their own musician roles within the band, songs and rehearsal schedule, resulting in a strong group dynamic which positively impacted on students and staff. Being members of the band gave the students a sense of purpose and belonging and their dedication inspired many other students to take up instruments. The school leadership team were impressed with the band's success and are now investigating further academic benefits of participation in the band.

Katy's research project focused on an increase in student numbers for the annual school play. While performing arts were generally valued by students and staff in her school, she felt that not all of the student groups were represented amongst the performers. How could she make drama accessible and attractive for all? After interviewing several focus groups, she decided that she particularly wanted to involve Year 7 students and girls of white British heritage in the next production. Traditionally these groups were the least represented in plays, resulting in a knock-on effect where whole friendship circles decided to take part in alternative activities rather than performing arts.

After approaching other tutors about her plan, many colleagues supported Katy by giving presentations to their tutor groups on the benefits of arts and culture, resulting in more than 200 applications for the production. The play 'Alice' by Laura Wade offered the opportunity for a large cast and throughout June and July, Katy was keen to give students the scope to act as autonomously as possible. An increase in attendance was not only noted in the numbers of performers and commitment to rehearsals, but both nights of the play's performance sold out to a more engaged school audience. When students reflected on their experience they particularly mentioned that they had felt pride in the production and that they had made new friends.

In summary, all three project leaders felt that the arts offered benefits to students who did not always have access to them. On their initiative visual art, music and performing arts enabled primary and secondary school children to increase their self esteem, collaboration skills and technical abilities. Allowing the students to take responsibility for some of their own learning further increased the children's sense of purpose and while originally it might have been increased participation in itself which was the target, the projects inspired many further benefits.

Our second set of research focuses on working across different departments within one school. Planning projects collaboratively brings its own challenges and opportunities, both for staff and students. How do we frame targets together and pursue their completion as a team, but in separate lessons? Can we work across the arts – and beyond?

Helen works at a school which holds the arts in high esteem and achieved Arts Mark Gold in 2016. The school's ethos focuses on Christian values and the leadership team was keen to introduce a cross-curricular Year 7 project which reflected this. The Lion King offered the opportunity to explore religious and artistic themes as well as providing other excellent educational resources. Helen did extensive reading before planning her project and together with colleagues from PE, Drama, RE and Music, she designed a curriculum which took place over the summer term.

Although Helen initially noted some uncertainty and hesitation from staff as the project began, she soon felt that it was easy to see the progress the different subjects were making and the teachers took more and more pleasure in working together. At the end of the summer term, the whole of Year 7 produced a show case, which was very well attended by the students and their relatives. Students took pride in their work and although Helen felt that it would ultimately only be possible to measure success in terms of GCSE arts subject uptake, she felt confident that the project had the potential to enhance transition from primary to secondary school and that the overall impact had been a very positive one.

Sophie planned to engage students and staff across the school in the development of a school garden. She was particularly interested in using the garden to increase engagement and attainment in students with low cultural capital. In Sophie's experience these students found it particularly hard to make links between subjects and they also did not feel as engaged in lessons. Based in London, Sophie's school boasts over 70 languages and a wealth of backgrounds and experiences; she felt that a garden project would be accessible to all students. With the help of a Gardener in Residence she established a timeline and identified students who would benefit from extra support and inspiration.

On the first of their project days, 210 Year 8 students were engaged in projects which combined Art, Design, History and Geography. As the success of the day became known amongst other faculties, Literacy, Maths and other Sciences started to plan their own gardening days, which promptly saw an increase in attainment and well-being. Throughout the project, Sophie monitored the number of teachers and faculties who were using the garden and particularly paid attention to individual students who benefited. At the end of the school year, all students and staff felt that the garden had made a positive impact and that they would benefit from its continuation.

Both of the cross-curricular projects paid special attention to the connection between different subjects but really came to life through the collaboration amongst staff from different departments and students from a range of groups. Working cross-curricular enables both teachers and children to make new social connections, learn skills and understand that most learning outside of school does not necessarily have a subject attached to it.

The third set of projects had the impact of research at its core. Three Cultural Leaders set out to focus not just on students, but on the research as a useful tool to measure progress, engagement and attainment. All three teachers used different methods and focused on a range of groups, from primary school children to SEN students and hard to reach pupils, yet all of them had the same goal in mind: to use action research to make an impact on their practice and develop as professionals.

Benjamin had previously seen the positive impact of using arts in the classroom, but was keen to produce some 'tangible results' which would illustrate these experiences. His school had identified spoken language as a key target for the following school year and Benjamin decided to use art work in lessons as discussion and conversation starters. He felt that art gave all children the opportunity to respond, whether English was their first language or not. Between March and July 2016, he introduced a different piece of visual art to the classroom every week. The class would discuss the piece for half an hour and Benjamin paid special attention to a supportive and friendly classroom environment in which all answers would be valued.

As the potential of the research was at the core of Benjamin's work, he made sure that the project was preceded and followed by a questionnaire, measuring the children's perception of their own contribution to the class and their confidence in discussions. He found that after the project, students felt they contributed more, listened better to others and felt like they were contributing their own ideas. Benjamin enjoyed the freedom of shaping his own research and data collection, but also looked at factors which limited his research. He felt that overall the research improved his ability to support the class and was keen to support colleagues with further action research projects in the future.

Elizabeth is a teacher at a community secondary school for students between 11 and 19 years of age who have severe and profound learning difficulties. As part of her project, she organised music workshops for three classes, one of which became her focus group. The workshops were delivered by Music Off Canvas, an organisation which provides interactive music workshops and it was hoped that they would provide the opportunity for the students to improve their communication, interaction and concentration skills. Similar to Benjamin's project, Elizabeth felt that the arts were accessible by all and she wanted to give students the opportunity to feel that they were active participants of the group.

The class consisted of six students, all of whom had very individual needs and attainment targets. Overall, research showed that the students were just as engaged (if not more so) during the music workshops and that they were able to participate. Elizabeth carefully outlined each student's progress as part of case study reports and commented on individual targets and development. Her attention to detail makes for fascinating and rich reading, paying attention to lots of different ways in which we can measure progress. She notes that it would have been useful to understand these individual targets before the research took place, but that the process had been fascinating and enriching.

Paul's project focused on the development of a research tool which would allow himself and his colleagues to assess and give insights on how to support individual development of their students. Based on the premise that a young person can only truly be engaged in the task they are involved in if their well-being needs are met, they created Engagement Profiles for three hard to reach students who were considered to engage more with the art room than their peers. These students were then monitored both in art and other subjects. It was concluded that the tool provided some useful insights, and findings were presented at the Royal Academy of Arts conference on creativity and SEN.

In summary, all three Cultural Leader found their research journeys challenging and rewarding. Being engaged in action research allowed them to look at their students from new perspectives through methods (or glasses) that they had constructed themselves. There is an unlimited number of ways in which we can assess progress and engagement, and which tool is best might indeed depend on the students and the particular context. Engaging in research offered the Cultural Leaders the freedom to explore new ways and to grow as professionals.

The fourth section of the book is concerned with Arts Award and its impact on students. Kerri, Yolanda and Rhiannon all took proactive and creative steps to increase the arts provision in their schools and to reward children for the artistic projects that they had engaged in. But are there other ways in which we can measure the success of Arts Award, apart from the award itself? What skills does the Arts Award foster and is it a qualification for all ages?

Kerri worked on a project which used the arts to encourage developing readers to engage further with books and reading. In January 2016, she created a group of 12 children aged 8 to 11 whose reading levels were two years under the expected development and encouraged them to come to a weekly after school club which had art as its focus. The aim was to award Arts Award Explore qualifications at the end of the project. Initially, students were reluctant to attend due to a lack of interest in the arts, but once Kerri had explained the literacy focus of the project, parents were more inclined to send their children. As part of the club, the children explored poems and books through the medium of art; drawing, printmaking and sculpture brought words to life and encouraged analysis.

In May 2016, all artworks were displayed in an exhibition and the children explained to their families which books their work was based on. All students received their Arts Award Explore accreditation in a whole school assembly and took pride in their work. Kerri worked with the children's literacy teachers to establish whether they had made the hoped-for reading progress and ten out of the 12 participants had improved their reading age between one and 25 months. Two children were now reading above their expected age range. While Kerri saw some limitations to the research, she saw substantial progress throughout the Arts Award project and felt that it had changed many children's perception of reading.

Yolanda's project focused on two groups of children. The secondary school students of her own school who were currently working towards a Bronze or Silver Arts Award, and several local primary school students in receipt of Pupil Premium funding. The primary school students were chosen to complete a Discover Arts Award programme, providing them with a slightly shorter route to a qualification. Together with her colleagues, Yolanda developed a framework which saw the collaboration of the two groups and particularly encouraged the children and their families to interact with a range of local arts on offer.

As an experienced leader of Arts Award delivery, Yolanda created workshop materials, collaborated with local art galleries and museums, supported the students and assessed the portfolios as they emerged. Collaborating with a range of very different primary schools was a feat of organisation and by involving her own school's students in the delivery of the programme, the benefits of the scheme spread all over the Waltham Forest region. Over the course of the project, 146 primary students achieved their Discover Arts Award and 26 secondary students won either Bronze or Silver Arts Awards. Yolanda felt that the project met and exceeded her expectations and was pleased that more local families were now aware of the rich cultural heritage of the area.

Rhiannon also focused on the benefits of the Discover Arts Award to Pupil Premium children. Working at an ethnically diverse inner city school in London with a creative curriculum, she is particularly proud to work in an environment which values the arts and hopes to apply for the Arts Mark Platinum in 2017. Arts are used across the school to engage students and Rhiannon planned a two week project for the three Year 2 classes which centred around the topic of 'Journeys' and included a trip to the seaside. In-class activities included literacy and visual arts and the children got to know a wide range of artists and practices.

The Discover Arts Award was completed by all children in Year 2 and the award was given out in a whole year assembly. Students also took part in a poetry recital and presented their work to friends and family. The 12 children of Rhiannon's research group felt that the project increased their self-esteem and all of them enjoyed the Arts Award journey. They could also name a wider range of artists and Rhiannon felt that the profile of the arts had been raised in her school.

Concluding, all three reports highlight the benefits of Arts Award both to primary and secondary school students. They provide fascinating discussions about the ways in which schools decide to run Arts Award programmes and the reasons why they engage with them. While children in receipt of Pupil Premium have been highlighted as a particular group of beneficiaries, the Cultural Leaders often make a point of stressing that there were little to no disadvantages of the Arts Award scheme. It seems that if a dedicated member of staff embraces the award, the leadership team and children will follow.

We hope that you enjoy the Cultural Leader reports. We encouraged all of our Cultural Leaders to include as many pictures as possible and we feel that these images add a real sense of the vibrancy of the arts and cultural projects.

INCREASING PARTICIPATION IN THE ARTS
Corelli College
City Year, Art and the National Gallery

Shermaine Slocombe

What is the impact of a creative project that focuses on personal development, confidence building, learning and behaviour? Will the participants in an arts project with a challenging cohort with multiple needs feel assured enough to express themselves to improve engagement, relationships, communication skills, confidence and behaviour and have the motivation to do more of the same?

As Arts College Manager at Corelli College, my role is to provide a sense of ambition for our young people by offering inspirational opportunities to enrich their lives. Creativity encourages participation, collaboration and co-operation, which form the heart of our community and the co-operative values our Academy is founded on. The arts bring genuine excitement, energy and colour to the life of our college and wider community. I provide opportunities for young people to work with dynamic organisations to support their learning and share their achievements. Through experience I know the likely benefits to students achieved through arts participation are confidence, emotional resilience, new skills, self-esteem, self-efficacy and improved relations between staff and students. I believe in the transformative power of the arts and how they make the world a better place, but often it is harder to convince others. The challenge was to measure the impact on a targeted group's understanding of the ramifications of their actions towards others and their motivation to take-up new possibilities and projects. Ultimately the goal is for them to join Corelli Arts Council – a group who meet weekly who have the power to make decisions and are given to direct access to high quality arts opportunities with huge benefits, both for themselves and the college.

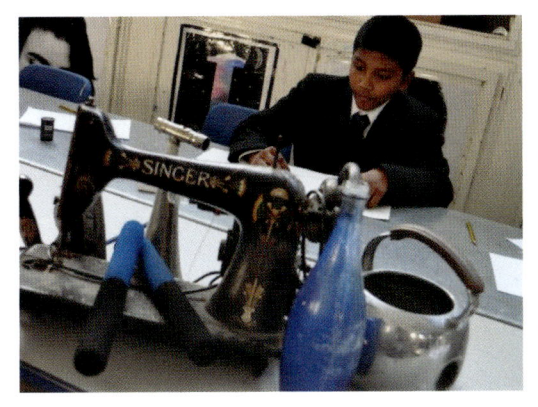

In 2016, Corelli College bought in the services of City Year. City Year is a group of young adults, aged 18–25 who help targeted students by creating positive near-peer relationships and act as positive role models to improve and increase students' love of learning. The young adult volunteers gain valuable experience in school and some go on to university or teaching. As a result of working with City Year, we were offered an opportunity to work with the National Gallery to introduce the students and staff from four schools to paintings so students would engage with their culture and heritage. The aim of the project was to enable students to connect with paintings and use the collection to enrich students' learning and their personal development. I knew this challenging project would be perfect for my research. City Year identified a small cohort of Year 7 students who liked art but needed extra support. They lacked confidence and had lower academic achievement that could lead to behaviour problems. The project took place from January until May 2016. Two Corelli staff and two City Year volunteers received training in December 2015. For staff, it was a luxury to analyse paintings, something we haven't done since our training. The four focus paintings were Caravaggio's *Supper at Emmaus*, Treck's *Vanitas Still Life*, Degas's *Miss La La at the Cirque Fernando* and Bellow's *Men of the Docks*.

In January we visited the gallery with the students to see the selected paintings. We discussed them in real depth, shared our responses and took part in practical workshops. The explorations and discussions in the gallery were a starting point for interpretations through workshops with artists, poets and teachers. The students experimented in printmaking, photography, drawing and poetry. Having had access to some of the world's most famous paintings, the aim was to inspire students to create their own responses and works of art during extracurricular time to be displayed in the National Gallery. We met once a week, every week. The students had to commit to lunchtimes and at times were off timetable to visit the National Gallery and finish their final pieces.

    These weekly sessions were led by myself, the head of Art and City Year volunteers. Initially, we had reservations about the students' attitude towards the works of art, but what grabbed their attention were not just the enviable skills of the artists, but the storytelling. Rather than having the symbolism revealed for each painting (because we really can't be sure of all the facts) they had to decipher it for themselves. We also kept the students on side by engaging in activities they found instantly rewarding and fun such as drawing. Nevertheless, this wasn't a bargaining tool, they were happy and realised very early on that they could creatively do what they wanted. I wasn't convinced they saw it as an achievement at this stage, but hopefully that would come. Having the input from the National Gallery was useful. Their approach was different to my mine. Whilst analysing paintings, experienced gallery facilitators at times bought out some deep emotions, enabling students to reflect on issues within their own lives. We also adopted techniques to engage students with these paintings. One student said *"It makes me feel the sudden urge of being somebody who explores and to find all the interesting objects between the timeline of life and death."* These sessions provided the students with a range of different ideas to build upon for our weekly sessions and their final outcome. The students identified very quickly that they wanted to make something new that was not in the world already.

    The joy for me was to run a project with no limitations; we were free to support the students to make what we wanted and to approach things in our own way. The National Gallery supported the project through outreach visits and follow-up visits to the gallery, but was never prescriptive.

Working with a somewhat hard to reach group of students had its challenges, particularly getting students to stick it out and appreciate the benefits. Due to the nature of the cohort, some students were excluded, left the project, couldn't attend, left to return to their country of origin or just couldn't commit to weekly sessions. We changed the time of the weekly sessions from lunchtime to after school; this had a big impact on numbers and helped with retaining the same group to build a relationship with. Doing the project over a long period of time was rewarding but it was sometimes difficult to maintain momentum and students joined the project who were not on our targeted list, but had heard about it and wanted to join anyway. We started with ten and ended up working with seven, but only three were from the original targeted list. Working with a core small group had its advantages and seven was a respectable number to work with to make a collaborative piece. However, inconveniently there is an Easter break and a bank holiday or an exam, and before you know it, a month has passed without seeing them. This is always the case in schools and always impacts on projects, no matter how experienced you are. I anticipated it would be as simple as collecting data and then analysing the results. Of course, in reality it doesn't always work out like that; staff leave and students leave. Students are generally better at drawing and ideas, rather than writing or doing something they perceive as traditional or academic. However, a benefit of doing a project over a longer period means there is time for students to trust you and build positive relationships.

Students were asked to complete an evaluation before and after the project. All three students of the target group were excited before the project, rather than nervous, scared or worried. In addition to the target group, a Year 7 Art class chosen at random was asked to complete the pre- evaluation. 95% of the class felt they were 'very confident' in trying new ideas and being in new situations, whereas out of the three target students, only student C believed them self to be 'very confident' and students A and B felt 'fairly confident'. The entire target group preferred working on their own, whilst only 9% of the class ticked this box. A and B felt they were 'good' at art and 66% of the class regarded themselves as 'good', 'very good' or 'excellent'. A felt they were 'poor' at performance and A and B certainly considered themselves 'not confident' in standing in front of people and working as part of a team. C felt it was 'somewhat true' that they were confident talking in front of people but felt 'certainly' confident to try new things. 76% of the class believed they were either 'good', 'very good' or 'excellent' at performance. 52% felt 'somewhat confident' standing in front of people and presenting their work and 29% believed they were 'certainly' confident. When asked to describe themselves in three words, the target group used words such as dancer, imaginative, happy and artist. When asked to describe what they hoped to gain from the project, the target group all agreed to have fun, make friends, be creative or gain confidence. The class in contrast self-assuredly described themselves as amazing, weird, smart, confident, good looking and funtastic!

> *"When we came to the National Gallery, we felt we wanted to know more about the paintings we were shown, which is why we have put so many objects and created a story for our final piece.*
>   *Objects that are different shapes and sizes, and details were important for our piece. They all symbolise something very different. We want you the audience to be curious about our work and ask questions – Leaving you wanting more.*
>   *We now know that no two artworks are the same and we wanted to use our imagination and make something new not in the world.*
>   *We wanted to try and recreate drama like in a film or in a dramatic EastEnders 'duff duff' moment. I think we have been successful. We hope you agree."*
> Student B

"Our story changed and developed over the course of the project and like most art; it can be whatever you want it to be! It all started when we put ourselves in the paintings. What was he looking at? He was looking at an extraordinary book that both evil and good were searching and hunting for. Within the book contained the map. The map revealed where the magic potion was.

The potion is powerful. Whoever drinks the potion has the power to transform people into monsters. The masked character found the potion first. His intention is to turn everyone into monsters and make the world evil. The character on the right didn't find the potion and is defending himself and humanity from being transformed into revolting monsters. Meanwhile. The guardian of the universe has the power. He breaks the 4th wall and is telling the audience to chill and be calm. He is all knowing and sees all, plus he can see into the future. The guardian of the ball has to destroy the earth to sacrifice for the greater good of the universe."

Student A

Teaching staff were asked to comment on the attitudes towards learning in their lessons before and after the project took place. Although there were not huge differences in the final results, of the three students who completed the project the teachers had noticed a difference in how they responded to others in the class. Their behaviour had not been affected by others in the class as could previously have been the case. They were now better at working in small groups, making fewer inappropriate comments and were less likely to distract others.

I watched them develop as artists because they were treated as artists. They gained confidence in trying new things like acting out scenes, being photographed and putting themselves in paintings. The group loved to draw and while they drew, they talked. They asked questions and I could ask students to reflect on what they had learnt. One student said *"Fascinating, I've looked at paintings I never knew existed. I have learnt to look deeper into the paintings and the value of living in the moment."* Their personalities shone through. I noticed how they perceived themselves and compared themselves to each other. For instance, student A recognised feeling envious of another student, due to their extraordinary drawing skills. They were at that stage in the project where they were yet to discover the many skills they possessed and had not yet acquired the new skills which would come over the course of the project. Asking student A to draw what they liked best about the project so far, they drew the group on a trip to the National Gallery. The same student also explained that they liked the sessions because they didn't get told off for saying crazy things; they could be imaginative, playful and inventive. This was a common statement made by all.

After the project, the three students completed the same evaluation to compare results. All three now were 'certainly' confident in standing in front of others, expressing their ideas, making new friends, trying new things and all believed they had learnt new skills and felt like a creative person. They all answered they were now 'very good' or 'excellent' at art and the same for performance. C now felt 'very confident' in listening rather than answering that this was 'not true' on the pre- evaluation. They all enjoyed teamwork and sharing ideas and being nice to people. When asked to describe themselves, they used words like designer, good reader, imaginative, creative and funny.

When asked what the best part of the project was, A stated *'I enjoyed working as a team and working as a small group, you were able to include everyone's ideas and it was a good practise at teamwork.'* B enjoyed the weekly sessions, proud to be chosen due to their interest in Art. B was most proud of speaking in front of an audience and visiting the gallery. C enjoyed the weekly sessions and drew this when asked to contemplate their favourite aspect midway in the project. In fact this was a highlight of the project for me – getting to know the students. They felt safe to question and challenge art, discuss art as a group, and had the confidence to share their opinions. I could appreciate them working as a team generating their storyboard, choosing which aspects would best represent their ideas as a final piece, especially knowing they all preferred at the start to work on their own.

In May, the project culminated in a celebration day at the National Gallery, which showcased students' final pieces and their diverse responses to the focus paintings. The final piece was presented in a meaningful and relevant way and that was important to the students; because of this it had a greater appeal and positive effect on their attitude to the project. Corelli staff were bursting with pride when our students nervously presented their final work to a very busy and intrigued National Gallery audience. Their work looked stunning and we were delighted in their achievement.

Inevitably all the students agreed they had learnt new skills and had an increased knowledge, and I could see the progression they made in listening and observing, but this feels harder to measure. I witnessed them respecting each other's ideas and opinions. The students learnt a lot about themselves and enjoyed making a collaborative piece of work. *'I have learnt to value art and I now know it is a way for me to express myself.'* The students now recognise they are great at drawing, inspired to draw, have incredible imaginations and are much more confident talking about art, *'I now know Art is everywhere.'* They feel proud of their achievements and I know it has fostered awareness of art for the future. *'Next time, can*

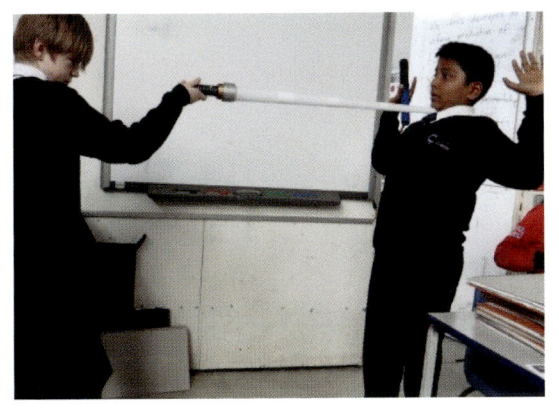

we go to a different gallery, so I can learn new stuff?' They gained an extraordinary appreciation of the art gallery and they definitely now can comprehend the works which belong to the nation, and that includes them.

They all confirmed they feel more confident in lessons, especially in art lessons, and as A said, they had achieved something special. B added that the key sources of enjoyment were because they made friends and loved working as a group and making a collaborative piece of art, especially using the photographic studio. A said they wanted to do it again and now understands art and has already taken their granddad to the National Gallery at the weekend. *'The best part though, seeing our work in the National Gallery that was pretty cool, I wish it could have been there longer. Next time, can we paint our final piece, rather than make a photograph?'* 'Um… maybe' I said, *'but I think we may need a few more sessions.'* B argued, *'But we liked the grandeur and the quality of the artworks in the gallery and we achieved that with photography.'* I quickly added, *'So, you would like to do it again then?'* A, B and C and all the others agreed. 'When is it?' they all asked.

See you at the next Corelli Arts Council session.

Kings Avenue School
Our school band

Savi Bale

Focus Area

This case study focused on increasing the provision of music for our gifted and talented children by forming a school band.

Aims

The aim was to help develop children's natural musical abilities by providing challenges, fostering independence, and encouraging them to engage with music emotionally and inspire others.

Background context and rationale

Kings Avenue School is based in Clapham, with a high percentage of children who qualify for Pupil Premium. The Arts became one of the curriculum drivers and thus had an increased importance within school life.

Over the years, Music had taken more of a focus in school life through regular singing assemblies, Arts Week activities, musical clubs, participation in festivals, external competitions/activities, toddler rhyme time sessions and more focused music lessons linked to the curriculum. Music lessons for children with special needs were successful, with the results showing increased concentration and confidence amongst the children.

With the increasing prominence and enjoyment of music it became clear that the musically gifted and talented children needed further opportunities to develop. The idea behind starting the band was to give the children an opportunity to develop their musical, collaborative and performance skills, have the opportunity to inspire others and to evolve the idea of a 'school band'.

The story

Prior research had shown that a very, very small percentage of children across the whole school regularly received private music lessons. Unfortunately, the school was not in a position to be able to offer children with fewer opportunities access to peripatetic teachers for individual lessons, as is commonly the case in many parts of the country.

> The Sutton Trust, an education charity, says that the richest fifth of households are four times more likely to pay for classes outside school than the poorest fifth of households.[1]

The children who were identified to take part in the project of starting the school band were a mix of children who received private music lessons and those who had demonstrated good musical ability in school lessons and performances. We wanted to try and have a mix of children across KS2 ages in order to foster social relations across the year groups, however, as the process developed, we were left with children from Years 5 and 6. We discovered that these children showed sufficient maturity, were willing to commit to the project and exhibited a real passion for music.

The rhythm section of the band, which consisted of two keyboard players, a bassist, drummer and two ukulele players were identified early on. The keyboard players had piano lessons (but not playing chords), the drummer and bassist were given opportunities to perform at church and were backed by encouraging parents and the ukulele players were good all round musicians within the school who regularly took part in all musical clubs.

However, finding a committed singer was a problem. The perceived pressure of being the centre of attention as lead

---

[1] BBC News. (2016). *Managing the cost of children's music tuition – BBC News*. [online] Available at: http://www.bbc.co.uk/news/business-29477202 [Accessed September 2016].

singer became an issue for those who auditioned and we tried to dispel the idea by offering to bring in more vocalists to ease the pressure.

Singing is a part of school life, yet to perform alone at a young age left children feeling vulnerable and unconfident. Although it is a fantastic chance for a talented singer to really develop and blossom, the fear that they would be laughed at put both boys and girls off joining the band.

> *'Some of the greatest challenges for music education in Western contexts concern how students' beliefs in their own abilities are shaped and change over time, and why so few are able to move from the initial sampling stage of experiencing music for fun...'*
>
> The British Psychologist Society[2]

I had, incorrectly, assumed that the confident, popular children, who had good tone and clarity to their voices, would be up for the challenge. However, our eventual vocalist was unassuming, with a powerful voice who had a real passion for singing. She was a Year 6 pupil who had provided a glimpse of her talent at a previous Christmas carol concert, but who also struggled with anxiety and a lack of self-confidence within school. I was able to work with her to overcome any fears and draw out her skills through individual sessions.

At around the same time, the band lost its original drummer. The children were proactive in trying to solve the problem, and our second keyboard player offered to try her hand at the drums. She had never sat in front of a full drum kit but began to play with ease and good rhythm. She practised regularly in the music room and with my help, was soon adapting various sections of the songs with different patterns and could make the transitions from verse to chorus very clearly, which helped the other musicians. Her

---

[2] Thepsychologist.bps.org.uk. (2016). *Motivating musical learning | The Psychologist*. [online] Available at: https://thepsychologist.bps.org.uk/volume-22/edition-12/motiv°ating-musical-learning [Accessed September 2016].

natural musical ability allowed her to be able to do this but without the introduction of the school band project she may never have discovered her drumming ability. This supports the idea that when challenged, children can use their existing musical skills to further themselves.

> 'As a performance skill, music is so multi-faceted and absorbing that its challenges seem limitless.'
> The British Psychologist Society[3]

Having assembled the band, the children and I listened to various songs to find songs that they all wanted to play. It was great to hear their thoughts on the musicianship of songs and whether certain songs were appropriate to represent them. They voiced their opinions with good understanding and musical language, for example, 'I can't play that riff' or 'those chords are too difficult'. They all agreed to play covers of well-known pop songs but said that they were also keen to write their own music in the future. Having decided on two songs to work on (*Counting Stars* by One Republic and *Hold my Hand* by Jess Glynn), the children were keen to get started with rehearsals.

Having provided the children with an initial questionnaire to discover their thoughts on forming a band and their individual strengths and weaknesses, there were common themes that ran through all responses. Most of the children were nervous about the challenge and performing in front of others (apart from the bassist), and were keen to learn new skills. Throughout the process, their different characters emerged as did the leaders and those who were content to take instructions. All children demonstrated good collaborative skills and in turn developed their timing and styles – the drummer and bassist became increasingly confident and experimental with their playing. Even with the good progress they had made, maintaining the children's

---

[3] Thepsychologist.bps.org.uk. (2016). *Motivating musical learning | The Psychologist*. [online] Available at: https://thepsychologist.bps.org.uk/volume-22/edition-12/motivating-musical-learning [Accessed September 2016].

enthusiasm and momentum was challenging, especially as it was sometimes difficult for them to visualise the end goal, and other commitments, such as SATs preparation began to clash with rehearsal time.

The children were keen to fix a date for a performance in order for them to have something to aim for. Over the coming weeks this group of children demonstrated dedication and motivation as they rehearsed together, often without being asked to do so by me. It was necessary for me to attend the rehearsals in order to guide the children to use their time efficiently. Being part of a band myself I was able to help them with chord changes, encourage them to perform their instruments in a way that complemented each other and in particular get them to have good eye contact with one another in order to create fluidity with their performance. It was clear that the children were enjoying their experience of being in a band and had formed closer friendships and a sense of purpose.

Although these children had been learning instruments and were involved in clubs, I felt it was important for the children to connect with music emotionally, through enjoyment. Whilst it has been documented that children who have had parental and teacher support to play an instrument are often successful and gain a sense of achievement by going through the examination process and receiving grades; without connecting emotionally to music, it is unlikely that children will continue their path in music with enjoyment and longevity.

The band performed on three different occasions to children, staff and parents and they were fantastically received and overwhelmed with their success. Having discussed their performances with them, the children were pleased with the outcome and eager to continue and develop further.

Outcomes and next steps

The creation of the school band has raised the standards of music within the school. Although music was prevalent in school life before the project, by involving our gifted and talented children and allowing them to share their talents, it has inspired and given confidence to many other children across the school. After the performances there was huge interest in learning an instrument and participating in the school band in future. The marked rise in passion for music in the school was noticeable and children were clearly inspired by what their talented peers had achieved. This was a good measure of the success of the project in terms of its effect on the school as a whole.

As for the musicians, they had developed their confidence in their own abilities, developed their reading and musicianship skills, become adaptable and aware of others, both musically and socially, and have been able to connect with the music they performed. As a result, they have all expressed a desire to continue the band outside of school.

The school leadership team had an overwhelming sense of pride and are keen for the band to continue as a platform for musically able children. They were aware of the 'school band', but did not realise how much hard work had been put in to it and the passion the children had for this project. They are now seriously investigating the correlation between the success of these children as performers and their academic learning.

Hampstead School
Through the looking glass – and what we found there

Katy Brown

Focus area

At Hampstead, we understand the power of Performing Arts, and what it does for our young people. I wanted to increase participation and explore the ways in which we could give more students an opportunity to lead in a range of roles both on and off the stage.

Aims

Since taking over the faculty in 2012, the whole school productions had been successful, highly praised and enormous fun to do. With a high turnover of staff, I often led projects such as this from the front. It was now time to empower the team to collaborate, and empower the students to have a voice, in a production that would ultimately be theirs. I wanted this whole school production to build on what we had done previously and explore what it could mean to re-invent the term, and be truly 'whole school' on a creative and cultural project.

The aim was simple. We hoped to achieve greater numbers of students taking part. Within this, we wanted to target particular underachieving sub-groups, and year groups where there were fewer students putting themselves forward and engaging in the cultural life of the school. Out of this came a second aim. To engage the staff in advocating for the arts and bring about a greater understanding of the benefit of participating in cultural activities for our young people.

Rationale

'It's great… but it's always the same faces'

This had been a piece of feedback given to me from a colleague after a summer production of *A Midsummer Night's Dream* in 2014, and had played on my mind ever since. Why did we have such enthusiasm for our subjects within lessons, yet we were not drawing a diverse enough group for our extracurricular work?

I decided to talk to my Year 11 GCSE Drama group about it. Out of 25 students, three had been in a school play. I asked them why they worked so hard on their Drama GCSE and were striving towards A grades, yet they hadn't ever put themselves forward in KS3 and taken part. Many explained that they felt they didn't have time outside of their schoolwork. This was not entirely surprising, however one student explained to me that for her, it was about 'Fear of missing out'. Missing out on socialising with friends, rather than doing this as an organised activity.

I wanted to find out more, and realised that their views would have to underpin the improvements I wanted to make. I wanted to use this research to develop our existing offer, and change our students' perception of cultural activities and the benefits they have.

Background context

Hampstead School is a larger than average secondary school. The proportion of students known to be eligible for free school meals is well above the national average. The students come from a wide range of socio-economic, ethnic, religious and cultural backgrounds. Most students are from minority ethnic backgrounds, the largest being of Black African heritage and any other White background. The proportion of students who speak English as an additional language is much higher than that found nationally. The proportion of disabled students and those with special educational needs is above the national average.

Ofsted report 2012

The Performing Arts faculty consists of eleven teachers, working across four subject areas (Drama, Dance, Music and PE). A range of qualifications are offered to accommodate all types of learners including GCSE, BTEC and Cambridge National Sports qualifications. GCSE Dance and Level 2 qualifications in PE form part of our core offer at KS4. Drama GCSE is regularly a popular option at Year 10 with consistently 40-50 students; there is also at least one group of level 2 BTEC Performing Arts in each of Years 10 and 11. Music has in recent years seen smaller cohort sizes at KS4 of around 10–15 students, however we have been able to introduce Level 2 BTEC Music to start in September 2016.

The Performing Arts at Hampstead are supported and celebrated regularly across the school and beyond. The majority of the team have been working at the school for four years or less, yet have successfully developed students' interests in our subjects and a range of links have been made with arts partners and freelance professionals in the delivery of content and in workshops and projects. There are annual (and termly) showcase events, and a range of extra-curricular clubs, concerts, performances and shows.

The Story

Our 2015 production of *Romeo and Juliet* had 40 students taking part. During this project we were surprised at the lack of Year 7 and 8 students taking part, leaving us with the majority of the cast from Years 9 and 10.

We wanted more students taking part generally, but also wanted to target Year 7 and 8 students or those with White British heritage.

How we did it

Gathering the facts: January –March

I don't get much free time, so when I do I just want to relax.

We began by surveying Year 9 tutor groups. The surveys asked them to highlight which 'cultural activities' they participated in regularly and asked them to provide reasons as to why they did or did not do them. There was an overwhelming divide between boys and girls, with most boys surveyed having a negative view of 'cultural activities' and not stating any other hobbies or interests either.

I would take part, because it looks very enjoyable, but I have other things that my parents want me to do.

From these surveys, smaller focus groups took place with those who did not participate. Some of the opinions mirrored what had originally been said by Year 11. Students felt that after schoolwork, homework and other responsibilities they did not have time. Students reflected on their lack of cultural awareness, and in particular did not know where to find clubs or projects within school and their local communities.

How can we change our daily habits and take part in cultural activities if we aren't told about all of them? Clubs outside of school are expensive, so the only experience I get is what school offers.

The majority of students interviewed explained that they enjoyed lessons, but unless their friends were involved in extra-curricular activities, they would probably not take part.

Taking part in the arts is good, because if you are not a confident person you can express yourself through creativity and show that you aren't only good at maths and science. I would take part if I heard more people talking about it, and saw more people doing it.

It was therefore, important to choose a project that would be wide reaching, but also give students the opportunity to participate in a range of roles or choose how much time they could offer. The act of taking part was the most important thing, whether on or off the stage. I realised quickly that it would be essential to explore student voice further in this production – and needed to build capacity within the team of staff in order to do this properly. The production needed to be much more visible to students (and staff).

Did you know that 70% of Oxbridge undergraduates have experience or qualifications in Drama, Dance or Music? Why do you think the top universities want students that have these skills?

Participate

Research shows that 70% of businesses believe extra-curricular activities make job-seeking school leavers and graduates stand out from the crowd. In addition, nearly two-thirds feel that candidates with such experience tend to be more successful employees and progress more quickly in their careers.

After discussions with Year 12 Theatre Studies students, we chose Alice by Laura Wade. A play with a large cast and design-heavy elements. Responsibility, reflection and resilience are themes that run central to Laura Wade's Alice. These are at the heart of our school ethos, and so this seemed the perfect choice.

The 'Participate' and 'Sign Up' campaigns: April–May

The next stage was to get the staff on board. After interviews with individual faculty members, a discussion around issues in cultural education across schools and London in particular was placed on the agenda at our Extended Leadership team meeting. Senior leadership, Directors of Learning and Heads of Faculty were presented with the findings of the in-school research so far, and a set of national (and local) statistics. It was no surprise that the team was resoundingly on board to support the project, and in particular the Directors of Learning in KS3 were keen to buck the recent trend in terms of their year group's levels of participation.

> It would be great to see more of our students having access to arts events from earlier on in the school and students more exposed to the opportunities they provide. Having the opportunity to go to more arts events is a crucial part of their education, which students from wealthier backgrounds often get through their families. I know that tackling this is not easy given curriculum constraints and that students and parents don't always see the point of such events, but I think such things are crucial in allowing students to see a world that is bigger than North West London
>
> Senior Leader

The tutor teams for each year group were asked to deliver a 20-minute presentation activity about the value of arts subjects and culture more generally, followed by discussions with their tutees about how participating at school can benefit not just university and college applications, but the whole person. At the end of the session and every morning that week, students were encouraged to 'sign up' as an expression of interest in either performing or production roles.

201 students signed up, with 120 wanting to perform in the production itself. 134 were from the target year groups, and we had a small but present group of white British girls!

Auditions and production meetings were held, and we were ready to begin the main part of the production process. During this time, we did see some decline in cast numbers, where some students lost interest or couldn't commit to enough rehearsals.

The production process, developing student voice: June–July

As the rehearsal process got underway, and after a Cultural Leaders session with Jan Polack from UFA, it became evident that deeper staff development was needed on student voice and student involvement.

Schools and organisations who give young people a voice and influence in learning have increased engagement of students, better attendance and behaviour leading to higher attainment. We also know leadership builds character with the ability to lead self and others, it deepens the learning experiences, and the skills developed are transferable.

UFA (University of the First Age)[4]

It was relatively simple to get the students to sign up. What became increasingly difficult with the pressures of time and resources was to ensure that we were able to allow the students the right level of autonomy in their production roles. A twilight training session was held with all teachers from Performing Arts, and Art and Design. Training was delivered using Hart's Ladder of Student Involvement, and team members were able to reflect on where on the ladder they were working with their designated groups. This training was a useful

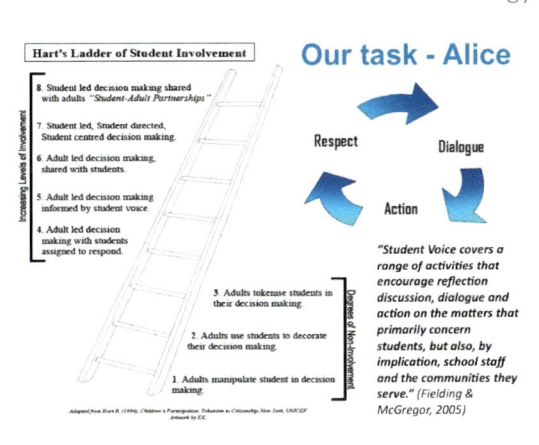

---

[4] Ufa.org.uk. (2016). [online] Available at: http://ufa.org.uk/ [Accessed September 2016].

chance to reflect on where we want to be in our future projects, and was also a great chance to evaluate what had been done.

Results and Impact

The impact of this project was very quickly identified as soon as we received the first sign up lists. Students who had never participated in extracurricular projects at school were attending after school every day. Many attended and stayed even if they weren't needed. Individual students, who had poor attendance, went to every lesson. Students who had chosen not to take part reflected on the idea that they may have 'missed out'. We began to see an unexpected change in the attitude of our wider school community. More students than ever were buying tickets to support their friends. Both nights were sold out.

There has been an increased staff awareness of raising the profile of the projects we run, and how if the students are empowered to lead, they are more likely to want to be involved.

The students involved wrote letters of reflection on the day of the dress rehearsal and we had overwhelming feedback from 100% of students that they will take part again.

Some student feedback:

Taking part has definitely been a big confidence boost for me.
Year 9

This has affected me in ways I didn't think of. I was able to build friendships, have more confidence in myself and was able to support other people. I will participate again for sure.
Year 9

Being in this play has been like being part of a brotherhood.
Year 9

I want to study medicine when I am older, and this play will show how hardworking and resilient I am. If I want to go to a good university I need to show that I participated.

Year 8

I think that other people should participate more too. Knowing there's a group of people who are always supporting you and helping you is a very nice thing.

Year 8

Being part of this has helped me out in my everyday life. In my lessons I have found that I am participating more, because I don't care what anyone thinks about me now.

Year 9

I wanted to impress my other teachers and show them that I can do more things… and trust me… I can! I have found friendship and fun.

Year 10

You are amongst a crowd of people who will tell you how to improve or what you could have done better, even sometimes when you don't want it. It's also somewhere where you feel appreciated for what you've done.

Year 9

My favourite part of this was coming here every day.

Year 8

I loved helping with the costumes and publicity and having the chance to show off what people had done, but I will sign up for acting next time.

Year 7

Thank you for letting me take part. The thing that made me stay was that I could be myself.

Year 7

It's made me feel like I have a responsibility. And there are so many talented people in Hampstead School

Year 8

Evaluation

The research process has been enlightening! In the early stages of the work, the feedback from Year 9 students (mainly boys) was brutal and forced me to take action. Having the opportunity to share the process of this research with my team and other colleagues has provoked some courageous conversations and will hopefully empower others in my team to build on what we have learnt. It would have been useful to gather more data from the students at more stages of the work, and run focus groups with those we still did not manage to reach.

Next steps

We have to build on what has been started. Key areas for development are:

- For all team members to evaluate the findings of this research and apply the key principles to further profile-raising creative projects.
- To reflect on the findings of this work in preparation for student pathways (Year 9 KS4 choices). Can we use this work to continue to grow numbers?
- Train staff in student voice more effectively and prepare for this in future projects.
- Continue to work with Directors of Learning and year teams to start a cultural morning as part of the 20-minute tutor period.

WORKING CROSS-CURRICULAR
Bishop Ramsey
A cross-curricular project between Expressive Arts and RE

Helen Simmonds

At Bishop Ramsey, specific subjects, even if they exist within one faculty area, often plan in isolation and deliver their curriculum individually. For instance, in the Expressive Arts Faculty, where there are four main subject areas, Art, Drama, PE and Music, collaboration only happens when an extracurricular event is being planned.

In addition there are very few opportunities within the main curriculum for cross-faculty planning. If, therefore, within faculties there is division in delivery and planning, can a cross-faculty project truly work? And what would be the benefits?

Context

Bishop Ramsey Church of England School describes itself as a Christian learning community. The arts are valued and nurtured at Bishop Ramsey and we have recently achieved Artsmark Gold. Leadership expressed an interest in the development of a cross-curricular project, which included Christian themes and values and the Arts.

A Year 7 cross-curricular project on 'New Beginnings' had been trialled two years previously, with limited success, generally because the project title was too loose, and because there wasn't sufficient collaborative planning. Furthermore, the students were unable to articulate the link between the subjects within the project, and although there was some good work in individual departments, it failed to meet the criteria of a cross-curricular project for both teachers and learners.

So why try it again?

Leadership had seen this work in other schools, which were similar in ethos to Bishop Ramsey. Benefits cited were smoothing transition from primary to secondary; profiling the work done in the arts and embedding Christian values within the pedagogy.

Literature supports the efficacy of such work. Statistics show that take up for arts subjects has fallen. Government policy seems to be steering us away from the arts, in terms of cuts to community programmes and the implementation of the EBacc. Could a large scale project, with an emphasis on creativity give students an incentive to study it further at GCSE and A level?

Current literature and ideas on the efficacy of cross-curricular work in schools, and the future of the Arts in British education

Much literature on current pedagogy suggests that where cross-curricular work has been implemented in secondary schools it has worked well. A paper documenting the effects of a Year 7 project, similar to the one we were going to undertake, stated that, *'The collective lesson time of all the participating subjects added together created a 'greater sense of purpose' for the Year 7 working a large scale project.'* Identity – a cross-curricular project Sam Eyre and Richard Marks.[5]

Studies have also shown cross-curricular project work to enhance thinking skills, which falls in with Constructivist thinking on pedagogy. The National Teacher Research Panel, for instance found that in this type of collaboration, *'There was an improvement in the quality of numerous areas of pupil learning, including: questioning, self and group reaction, sharing of ideas, consensus and awareness of task requirements.'*[6]

---

[5] Nsead.org. (2016). *NSEAD.* [online] Available at: http://www.nsead.org/home/search.aspx?s=identity [Accessed September 2016].

[6] Price, A. (2010). *What are the benefits for teaching and learning of cross-curricular work using thinking skills, techniques and language?* [online] Available at: http://www.ntrp.org.uk/sites/all/documents/A.%20Price%20FINAL.pdf [Accessed September 2016].

Additionally, in *Cross-Curricular Based Learning* by Whitney Hoffman,[7] the rationale behind projects like these were to give learners – in particular those who found factual learning difficult, *'additional "cognitive hooks" that enhanced their mastery of skills while also helping them with social skills and an alternate way of demonstrating their knowledge.'*

Other literature worked to debunk the idea of cross-curricular work, particularly where the emphasis was on collaborative group work. For instance, Kirschner, (1992) disagrees with the two main assumptions underlying constructivist theories: that they *'challenge students to solve 'authentic' problems or acquire complex knowledge in information-rich settings,'* and second, that *'they appear to assume that knowledge can best be acquired through experience based on the procedures of the discipline.'*[8]

However, real world learning has become a buzz word in education and learning how to learn is seen as a progressive, holistic approach.

The project we were to undertake, had a second purpose, the evidence for which will not be available until March 2017 and onwards. *Arts Professional* for June 2016 states that:

'Entries for GCSEs in arts subjects have fallen by 46,000 this year compared with last, according to new figures recording England's exam entries for 2016. The drift away from arts subjects is gathering pace. This year's loss is more than five times the size of the loss in 2015, when candidate numbers fell by 9,000.'[9]

The Guardian also reported that:

'Some of the most striking statistics are around education. Between 2003 and 2013 there was a 50% drop in the

---

[7] Edutopia. (2016). *Cross-Curricular Project Based Learning*. [online] Available at: http://www.edutopia.org/groups/project-based-learning/597671 [Accessed September 2016].

[8] Kirschner, P.A. (1992). *Epistemology, practical work and academic skills in science education*. Science and Education, 1, 273-299.

[9] ArtsProfessional. (2016). *EXCLUSIVE: Arts in schools plummets, new figures show*. [online] Available at: http://www.artsprofessional.co.uk/news/exclusive-arts-schools-plummets-new-figures-show [Accessed September 2016].

GCSE numbers for design and technology, 23% for drama and 25% for other craft-related subjects. In 2012–13, only 8.4% of students combined arts and science at AS level. The number of arts teachers in schools has fallen by 11% since 2010 and in schools where a subject has been withdrawn, drama and performance has dropped by 23%, art by 17% and design technology by 14%.[10]

These are scary figures, both for the rounded, cultural education we are passionate about and for the future of our careers.

The project

We chose *The Lion King* as the cross-curricular 'story'. We chose this for a number of reasons:

- It is a current West End show and this would give every child an opportunity to travel to London to see a live theatre performance.
- There are excellent educational resources on the website, plus a film about the production which would give students an enriched experience at the theatre.
- The themes are excellent for RE and Drama.
- The study of African music is already a small part of the Music curriculum.
- The project provided ample opportunity for 3D, mask making and colour work in art.
- It is a popular film and therefore a familiar story and concept to the Year 7 learners.

The project would be collaborative, but led by the Heads of the Arts and RE Faculties. Within that, each department would develop their own approach to the project, including homework tasks. It was decided that no one department

---

[10] Brown, M. (2015). *Arts and culture being 'systematically removed from UK education system'.* [online] the Guardian. Available at: https://www.theguardian.com/education/2015/feb/17/arts-and-culture-systematically-removed-from-uk-education-system [Accessed September 2016].

would spend longer than a term or less than half a term on the work.

We chose the summer term for our project, however PE would have to do the project in the Autumn Term due to restrictions on space and other ongoing commitments. For the most part work would be practical, with elements of debate and research.

The project would be framed by a launch during an assembly where each of the departments spoke to the whole year group about what the project would entail. We then took all the year group to the West End production and in classes we showed some of the educational material around the staging and costuming of the Julia Taymor production.

The final outcome would be an evening where parents, carers and families could come and watch the performance and look at the art work produced by the students. This would be an informal early evening event lasting around an hour.

Limitations on the delivery of the project and accuracy of the findings

Any concrete impact on the perception of the arts can only be measured by the uptake at GCSE level, and this would be two terms on from the project (options are decided in term 2 of year 8). Also the impact could only be measured by comparing it to previous years, during which the negative effects of the EBacc and Government policy was less pronounced.

We looked at the model used by Coombeshead College however their project involved 'Impact Days' where the project was embedded, which was something we couldn't implement at Bishop Ramsey due to the fact that Curriculum Days were already planned a year in advance.

The College also used the idea of project folders to keep the students' project in one area, which was something we decided against due to budget constraints and a general feeling that the identity of the subject might be lost. It was also felt to be impractical due to the time restraints on the different subject areas.

So what were the outcomes?

The curriculum

As with every new initiative, there was a mixture of excitement and uncertainty from the staff. For each member of staff there were different challenges. For some it was the showcase and the idea that work by Year 7 students would be on public display. For others it was simply changing a well known KS3 scheme of work to a different one at a time when change at GCSE and A level was a whole school focus. For all of us it was collaborating on a project after years of working on curriculum individually.

Once the project was underway, however, uncertainties lifted. In Art, as the masks and 3D animals were on display in the art rooms throughout the project it was easy to see the progress. It gave the department a KS3 focus for any visitors to their rooms. The 3D animal work was a great success, considering the teacher who led this was at first reluctant.

In dance, the students were excited and enthused throughout the project. There was an issue, however in that the dance work was done in the Autumn Term, meaning that work had to be revived for the showcase. This caused some worry from some in the Department that the students would not want to revisit work they had already done, however this was not the case. The dance work was excellent and received a great deal of praise from the audience members.

In drama the students enjoyed the project immensely, many stating that the *Lion King* project was their favourite of the year, although, midway through the project there was some uncertainty amongst students as to how the project tied together. For instance, some of the drama work was about using the animal kingdom to tell stories. We looked at Aesop's Fables for this. We also used Shakespeare to deliver the themes of the Circle of Life (7 Ages of Man).

After the project was finished the teachers expressed their enjoyment at working together but conceded that we could have collaborated more in the middle of the project instead of mainly focusing on the planning and the end product.

The showcase

The showcase, which was the climax of the project, was a success. Despite the fact that an important European Cup football match was being broadcast that afternoon, we had almost 100% attendance. Also, there were over 150 parents/family members who came to view the art and watch the showcase.

Because the event wasn't ticketed, we were initially surprised by the attendance of so many audience members. This also had an impact on space (we had chosen the Hall as our venue) and it meant that the voices in the drama work couldn't be heard at the back of the audience.

The art work was displayed outside the Hall area and it looked spectacular. Each student's name was put next to their piece. There was a very obvious sense of pride in the work as students took their parents/carers and siblings around the work.

The dance pieces were spectacular. It had been decided that only some groups would show this work even though all students had taken part in the lessons.

Music was two songs sung by all the students. This was performed in the middle of the showcase and at the end. It was both moving and heart warming to see the young people swaying and joining hands for the songs. There was a tangible sense of identity and inclusion in this part of the showcase.

Discussion immediately after the showcase was very positive. It was decided that the showcase was a success, in that it provided a sense of pride, unity and achievement. It also allowed the families of the students to view the work of the young people and be involved in it. We all felt that technical issues such as using microphones and planning the floor space would be achievable in the future. We also discussed ways in which we could plan more effectively for audience numbers.

What are our next steps?

There are three ways forward for this project:

- Run the project in exactly the same way as in 2016.
- Go back to working as individual departments.
- Refine and develop the project for future years.

After discussion it was decided that the project will now run on a regular basis. It will remain a summer term project. We will regulate our homework policy within the project; use differentiation and refine the way we run the showcase.

In a year we will start to measure the uptake in arts subjects. We hope to be able to understand whether this project has any influence on the uptake of arts subjects. It might also be used to enhance transition from primary school, where project based work is the norm, to secondary – in which case there might be a change to the timing of the project. This will mean that Year Heads, Pastoral Staff and Form Tutors will all be involved in the project.

Hampstead School
The Concrete Garden

Sophie Rodger

Focus area

Through the introduction of a garden we hoped to investigate the impact of hands-on, cross-curricular learning on the attainment and engagement levels of students with low cultural capital[11] in a secondary school context.

Aims

We hoped to increase students' levels of attainment through practical learning and engagement by providing access to an alternative learning environment. Our plan was to create an interdisciplinary space for the practical application of classroom learning and to empower students to design, build and nurture a learning environment of their own. We hoped that the garden would act as a connection between all the subjects within the Art & DT Faculty and help to contextualise learning.

We hoped that through the creative process of planting, watching, waiting, growing and tasting, students would experience learning in a more holistic way. We hoped that the garden would provide an access point for students to encounter a range of artistic, environmental and creative experiences hence providing them with cultural capital opportunities.

[11] In this report, cultural capital is defined as exposure to and engagement with a range of artistic and creative experiences.

Rationale

I had become increasingly aware that students find it hard to make links between subjects even when they are learning the same thing. This seemed to be especially true among those students who had low cultural capital. This limited understanding of the wider world stifles students' learning and their ability to make links. It also leads to lower levels of engagement within the classroom. I observed:

- many students with low cultural capital in the school.
- issues with levels of engagement and engagement in classroom lessons.
- a potential correlation between levels of engagement, and levels of cultural capital/contextualised learning.

Background context

Hampstead School is a larger than average secondary school in Camden. The proportion of students known to be eligible for free school meals is well above the national average. The students come from a wide range of socio-economic, ethnic, religious and cultural backgrounds. Most students are from minority ethnic backgrounds, the largest groups being of Black African heritage and any other White background. The proportion of students who speak English as an additional language is much higher than that found nationally. The proportion of disabled students and those with special educational needs is above the national average.

Our students are breathtakingly diverse with over 70 languages spoken and a wealth of backgrounds and experiences. They are talkative and demanding, they expect teachers to expect them to succeed. Our students are fun, frustrating and surprising.

A huge building project began in September 2015, which reduced our outdoor space significantly. The idea of the garden was initially to link the four subjects (Art, Photography, Design Technology and Food Nutrition and Preparation) within my faculty together. We also hoped to create a softer, more pleasant outdoor space to offset the 100 lorries entering the site every day!

Hampstead School has an incredibly committed staff team who worked hard to minimise the disruption that the building work could have on learning. The day is split into five hour-long lessons, often doubles to avoid movement around the school. Due to the lack of space our lunchtime has been reduced to half an hour. Students spend break times in year rooms, playing table tennis or sitting chatting in various hiding holes around the school buildings.

The story

Having two children in an inspiring primary school where 'projects' provide a context for learning and allow them to explore a wide range of subjects, I became frustrated with what secondary schools have to offer. It is no surprise that there is a well known dip in learning for students who transition from KS2 to 3 as learning is restricted to subject areas and students stop making links and start to compartmentalise their learning.

As an art teacher I was also aware of the difference in the ability of students who had cultural capital and those who did not to make links, experiment with ideas and draw on prior knowledge in order to push their creativity to exciting outcomes.

Project based learning does not tend to work well in secondary schools due to structures, time and resources. Our challenge was to provide a learning resource that could be used by the whole school that would help to contextualise students' learning and allow students with low cultural capital to develop some.

How we did it

As Head of Art & Design Technology I look for an Artist in Residence each year. This year I found more than I hoped for when I met Susannah Phillipson, (Gardener in Residence) an outstanding educator who has turned this project from a nice idea to a new way of looking at secondary education. She has made some of the best parts of primary school project based teaching accessible to a secondary school environment. Susannah worked three days a week for two and a half terms.

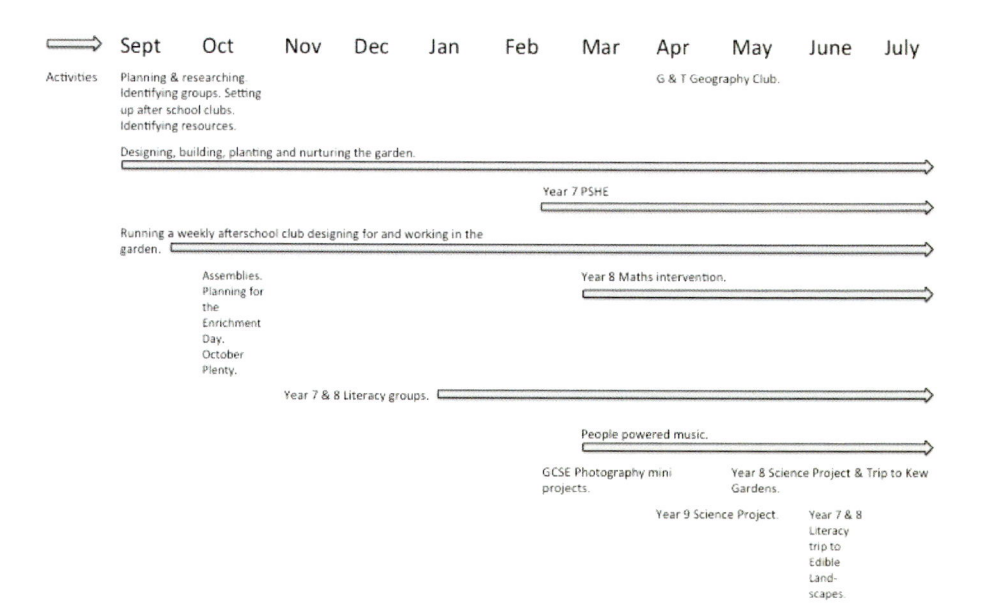

Activities	Sept	Oct	Nov	Dec	Jan	Feb	Mar	Apr	May	June	July

Planning & researching. Identifying groups. Setting up after school clubs. Identifying resources.

G & T Geography Club.

Designing, building, planting and nurturing the garden.

Year 7 PSHE

Running a weekly afterschool club designing for and working in the garden.

Assemblies. Planning for the Enrichment Day. October Plenty.

Year 8 Maths intervention.

Year 7 & 8 Literacy groups.

People powered music.

GCSE Photography mini projects.

Year 8 Science Project & Trip to Kew Gardens.

Year 9 Science Project.

Year 7 & 8 Literacy trip to Edible Landscapes.

We initially had funding for one term but due to the success of the project our funding was extended until the end of the academic year. The project developed intuitively by responding to the needs of students and staff.

We started by creating a garden. We identified groups of students to work with, and through after-school sessions started to up-cycle and design planters. This time line outlines the key events throughout the year.

At the end of the first half term we used one of our school 'Enrichment Days' to engage the whole of Year 8 (210 students) with the garden. The day was called 'Change, Mutate, Grow' and the Art & Design Faculty worked with Social Sciences to plan a range of workshops in which activities brought Art, Design, History and Geography together through looking at plants. We were fortunate to benefit from a team of volunteers who brought skills such as bread making, mosaic designs and permaculture.

The day was a huge success in terms of engagement and the garden took root.

The day also set the tone for this project. The garden could provide a real life context for all subjects to connect to.

More and more Faculties started to ask to work with the garden. The Art & DT garden was now at the hub of Literacy, Maths, Science and Geography. It provided extension tasks for our more able students and subject matter to engage those who found concentrating difficult.

This project used plant growing as a tool for integrating students' learning, providing an insight into the interdisciplinary possibilities of subjects and developing practical skills and discourse around food production. It also enhanced students' attainment through group project work, and increased wellbeing in the school environment.

Working closely with all areas of Art and Design Technology, we designed and built growing systems – with students – around and within the learning spaces. We observed the process of growing, cooking from the harvest and explored the artistic potential of plant cultivation.

Throughout the project we worked in collaboration with students to facilitate their ideas and to practically apply the curriculum to a hands-on project outside the classroom. Alongside the main cultivation process, we ran a half-termly programme of after-school activities for all ages and enrichment projects for Sixth Formers, with support from outside practitioners.

Staff were invited to work with Susannah to plan sessions for their students. The following groups worked closely with the Concrete Garden:

- Literacy Year 7.
- Literacy Year 8.
- Geography G&T (Y7-9): 4-week practical research project into the history and geopolitics of plants and food production.
- Maths Year 8: Hands-on learning about volume and area, using compost and containers to get a visual and kinaesthetic understanding of space, measurements and proportion.
- Photography Year 11: GCSE coursework photography, looking at patterns in nature.
- PSHCE Year 7: Student-led design project, in collaboration with Biomodd London.
- Science Year 8: A 4-part chilli-growing project, extending through the summer term.
- Science Year 9: Designing renewable energy systems: wind power, solar power, bicycle power.
- Lunchtime and After School Club: The After School Club provides a space for students to explore the garden in their own time, and to develop all the skills relevant to creating a growing space.

Quantitative data has been difficult to collect this year as we have been designing and developing the project in response to students' needs. However there are a few clear examples of students' progress improving due to their time working on projects based in the garden.

Results and impact

The outcomes of the intervention are based mainly on observations and qualitative information and can be summarised in the following points:

- Students' engagement with their learning improved.
- Students started to make greater progress than expected.

- A platform for teachers from different subject areas to share ideas and plan together was created.
- A lifeless part of the school developed into a surprisingly beautiful area.
- Vulnerable students found a space to make friends and develop social skills.
- The way staff and students thought about teaching and learning started to change.

At the beginning of the project we gathered data about how engaged a group of Year 7 students felt and how many links they could find between different subjects. We hoped to compare this data to data collected at the end of the project. This data was not robust enough to show anything significant.

A more significant way of measuring our success was by monitoring the number of teachers and represented Faculties that used the garden as a resource. Initially the garden was designed to bring cohesion between the subjects in the Art & Design Technology Faculty. We did not imagine the extent to which it would engage teachers and change the way they taught.

In September 2015, only the Art & DT Faculty were using the garden as a resource.

In October Social Sciences got involved. Achievement Support was quick to join and used the garden significantly throughout the year. Science and Maths found engaging ways of utilising the space. By the end of the year all 8 Faculties had engaged with the garden in one way or another. Half of all the Faculties were using it regularly in a significant way that changed the way they taught their subjects.

Did we manage to improve students cultural capital in any way through their experiences in the garden?

While the project began with humble intentions, it has demonstrated itself to be a vital resource for our teachers and students, with many great success stories that have transformed students' life opportunities. The cultural capital in which students improved was not an exposure to great art forms, but an experience of taking risks and trying new things in order to learn, which you could argue is the first step towards this.

Our school has changed in many ways through the creation of the Concrete Garden; on the surface it has created a welcoming and engaging environment for students to develop and apply their learning both in and out of lessons and to make friends through a practical project. The space has been respected from the start with no incidents of littering or vandalism with many students taking responsibility to not only protect it but also to actively engage their friends in what they have learnt.

The project has got staff talking to each other and has aided teachers in finding different ways of teaching, making lessons more practical and more hands on.

Here are a few stories of students who have directly benefitted and feedback from teachers who have used the Concrete Garden:

Case Studies

Student 1 in year 7 has worked with his Literacy group in the garden this year. At the beginning of the year, he was easily distracted and demotivated. His lack of engagement resulted in very low literacy levels, which in turn led him to distract others. He engaged more in the garden than anyone else. This, combined with his literacy lessons has resulted in a huge improvement in his reading age – an increase of five years one month. For the first time in his life he has become an expert (he can tell you the names of all the plants in the garden) with real career opportunities.

Student 2 in year 11 had low expectations of himself with a Hampstead Target grade of D+ for Photography. He has literacy and numeracy difficulties, difficulties with phonological processing, logic and inferential reasoning. Through working with Susannah in the garden his engagement in photography increased and he was able to grow in confidence resulting in a C grade at GCSE.

Student 3 also has difficulties with literacy and keeping a clear focus. He also exceeded expectations for his coursework in photography achieving a C grade – the only subject in which he achieved this.

Student 4 (a young man with very complex needs) has benefitted in a number of ways from getting involved in the after school club. He is now able to start a conversation appropriately and develop it to an extent, maintain eye contact and wait his turn. He has also benefitted from interacting with the other students and he says himself that he has made friends. He enjoys going to the garden because he has nice friends there and views it as a safe haven.

Feedback from teachers who used the Garden:

It has been really useful to show real world uses of multiplication as applied to length, area and volume with something concrete as they find it hard to conceptualise numbers, processes and values. Behavior is tricky so having something that is hand-on has been brilliant.

Maths

Pupils who are quiet and withdrawn in the classroom become enthusiastic, helpful and confident learners. Susannah is a very capable, unflappable and gifted teacher – she involves the students very actively in learning and relates this to science, nature and the ideas entailed. Pupils can see, feel and touch the plants which they tend, direct experience is linked to knowledge of underlying concepts, they learn about plants, horticulture, biology and botany and, most importantly, in the process become active developers of the school environment. They develop skills of dexterity, co-ordination and judgment as they help.

Achievement Support

During this project I have worked with two small classes of students in literacy classes in years seven and eight. In class many of these students display diffident and defensive behaviour – they are not yet confident learners. When they go to work with on the Garden Project they transform into being eager, curious and highly energised. They compete to be given responsibility – all defensiveness vanishes.

Susannah

We asked some students who had taken part in the Year 8 chilli growing science project, to fill in a questionnaire.

This is a summary of the feedback:

- 100% of students agreed that it has been helpful learning through a project rather than individual lessons.
- 96% of students said that growing the chilli plants has helped them engage with their learning more.
- The class identified eight other subjects that this science project linked to, including Literacy, Geography, DT, PSHCE and Maths.
- Over half the group said that they are motivated in class by learning that's relevant outside the classroom.
- 74% of students said that they felt more motivated doing this project than they normally do in science.
- 89% of students think that they'll remember what they have learned about soil, minerals and plant development more, having grown the chilli plants.

When asked in what way this project has been different to their other learning in science, they said:

- More practical and more linked with the outside world.
- Practical lessons are easier to understand.
- We don't normally do so much group work in science.
- It is different because you can fully understand how the project works, through the experience of seeing how the plant is affected.
  I can take what I've learned into my daily life.

100% of students asked think the Concrete Garden Project should continue at Hampstead School. When asked why, they said:

It helps children experience more stuff about plants.

It makes everyone take care of the environment much more.

It improves my experience at school and makes me feel as if I'm helping the planet. It also makes our school stand out to others.

It shows you what actually happens to plants in industrial farming, and what people are eating.

It gets me involved in science more because it makes me more interested.

It gets people involved in groups and group-work.

It gives us a broader understanding of our environment.

We get a clearer understanding of how science works.

It's fun. Not only that but it helped us understand what different elements do to the plant and to the human body.

Because you learn how much plants affect you and the food chain.

Miss Phillipson tries to involve everyone and makes it fun – like riding a bike to make a radio work.

It's good to experience the project rather than just learn it.

It has taught us about gardening, minerals, and about growing plants.

Growing food is often neglected and not learned about in school. Through the Concrete Garden Project we can learn things we otherwise wouldn't, and be cautious about our planet.

Evaluation

The Concrete Garden Project was motivating, exciting and we watched it change the atmosphere of the school. This report however is really my observations of how the school changed as a result of the project. As a research project I was not clear enough at the beginning with what I wanted to find out and so my baseline data collection was too vague. It is frustrating now having got to the end of one year to not have solid data to push for further funding.

If I had had time at the end of the school year, I would have liked to interview a wider range of staff and students to get broader feedback on the project and how it affected them. The next piece of research I do will have a smaller and much clearer aim. I would probably also prefer to measure impact over a longer period of time in order to really see how different interventions impact on staff and students' learning and experience.

Next steps

Our plans are to develop this project further. We have distributed many of the day-to-day garden responsibilities throughout the staff team in order to keep the project running if we are unable to sustain our funding. I would like to work with the teaching and learning team in order to look at the Year 7 curriculum and their transition from Year 6. If possible we could create a more joined up curriculum based on the garden.

If we are able to secure funding for Susannah for another year we would like to develop the space further and create another student-led area in the form of a Geodome powered by sustainable energy in which to perform music and explore lighting and space. This in turn could be used to challenge and develop teaching and learning across the school.

ACTION RESEARCH AS PROFESSIONAL DEVELOPMENT
Mayflower Primary School
The use of visual arts to increase children's confidence in spoken language and discussions

Benjamin Jones

Aims

I have used artwork throughout my teaching career in many different contexts: to generate questions, to enthuse students at the beginning of a topic or as a stimulus for writing. My experience of using artwork in the classroom is that it is a valuable resource which all children can relate to in some way or another. When presented with a painting, for instance, children are much more likely to have something to say because it is open to interpretation. Through this piece of research I hoped to achieve some tangible results which would show how the arts can improve and enrich children's experience in school. I also hoped to show how the arts could develop skills in different areas of the curriculum.

Rationale

The school had identified spoken language as a key area for development and it was part of the school improvement plan. P4C (Philosophy for Children) was introduced at the beginning of the year to begin to develop children's spoken language in discussions.

P4C encourages children to learn through enquiry and the exploration of ideas. A session often begins with children developing questions in response to a stimulus. The group then chooses a question to discuss together. There is an emphasis on community building so that all members of the group feel included and all contributions to the discussion are equally valued.

I wanted to show that using the arts in different contexts across the curriculum could be exciting, stimulating and valuable to children and teachers. This was my starting point.

I decided to use artwork as a stimulus for P4C discussions with my class. My experience had been that children respond positively, creatively and enthusiastically to the visual and immersive nature of art. It is a leveller – everybody can have something to say, there are no right or wrong answers. The use of a visual stimulus was also inclusive in a class where most children spoke English as a second language.

Background

Mayflower Primary school is a 1½ form entry school situated in Tower Hamlets, in the East End of London. 55% of our students are eligible for free school meals and 97% speak English as an additional language. We have a dedicated and enthusiastic staff team who are always striving to develop and improve the school. We also place a big emphasis on collaborative working across all members of the school community. Mayflower has a creative, topic based curriculum based around a diverse range of books and stories. Every class is named after an artist and we begin each year looking at and investigating their work. We use our location in London to make the most of the museums and galleries through regular trips across the year.

The Story

The school had identified spoken language as an area for development. We wanted all our students to feel confident speaking to others in class and in assemblies but also in their wider lives. Through developing the students' spoken language we hoped to give them confidence in discussing, debating and questioning other's views. P4C has been shown to address many of these issues through regular class discussions. All staff at the school received training at the beginning of the year and it was introduced across the school. I was also keen as the art co-ordinator at the school to develop ways for staff to engage with the arts and culture across the curriculum.

How we did it

I decided to use artwork as a stimulus for the weekly P4C sessions in my class. I hoped that using art as a vehicle for developing children's speaking and listening skills would be especially effective.

The intervention took place over five months from March to July 2016. At the beginning of March I gave the students an initial questionnaire containing six statements:

When we have a discussion in our class, I contribute.
I feel confident talking about new and unknown ideas.
When I contribute, I speak in sentences.
I find listening to other children's ideas interesting.
When I listen to other children, I want to respond with my own ideas.
Discussions make me more interested in my learning.

The students responded to each statement by ticking one of four words (Never, Sometimes, Usually, Always). As the students were 6/7 years old, I read each statement out to the class and time was given for them to respond.

For the following five months, we had a weekly discussion for half an hour based on a reproduction of an artwork displayed on the whiteboard. I chose the pieces carefully to reflect the current learning in the class. For example, during a week where the class were investigating and writing about the Galapagos islands we looked at the Peter Doig painting *100 Years Ago* which depicts a canoeist in front of a distant island.

The sessions followed a specific structure including warm up activities, 'thinking time', generating questions and a discussion for around 15–20 minutes. There was always an emphasis on every student's contributions being valued and there being no right or wrong answers. I encouraged students to respond to each other with sentences starters such as 'I agree/disagree because…' or 'I want to build on…'

At the end of July, the class completed the questionnaire again to measure any change.

Results and Impact

As a result of the intervention I put in place there were several significant changes which became apparent when analysing the data collected from the questionnaires:

- Before the intervention 19% of the class felt they always contributed to discussions in the class. After the intervention this rose to 69%.
- 29% of the class always found listening to other children's ideas interesting before the intervention. This rose to 56% afterwards.
- Initially, 19% of students always wanted to respond with their own ideas when they listened to other children. At the end of the intervention this rose to 38%.

When I began to examine the data I saw a pattern emerge which showed a general shift towards students answering the statements on the questionnaire from 'never/sometimes' to 'usually/always'.

This project provided me with the evidence and incentive to develop the school's use of the arts and culture across the curriculum. Over the coming year I will be adding suggested artists and artwork to the school's creative curriculum. For each topic across the year, teachers will have a bank of images or other resources that they can use as stimuli for discussions in P4C and other activities.

Evaluation

Having not produced research previously, I found the process exciting and engaging. It developed skills I would not usually use in day to day teaching. Reflecting and improving the different elements of the research project (planning, data collection etc.) gave me the most satisfaction. It has been an important opportunity for me to add to the evidence of the importance of arts and cultural education in schools.

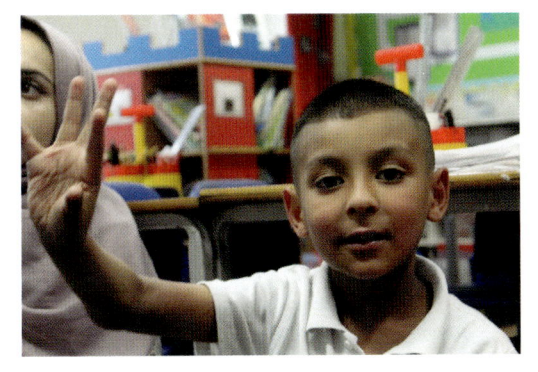

The research process was simpler and less technical than I expected and I enjoyed the freedom of choosing my own methodology and forms of data collection. Through the process I began to understand the importance of the conclusion and findings – reflecting on strengths and weaknesses in the research and acknowledging other factors that may have influenced my findings.

There were inevitable challenges with fitting the intervention into my teaching week. I also found it difficult keeping the profile of the project at the forefront of my mind, with all the other elements of the job. Initially I also found it challenging to find an appropriate data collection method that would accurately reflect impact. However, with support I was able to create and test a questionnaire so it would be most effective.

I was also aware of the possibility of bias in the research. If I believed that the intervention I was running was going to be successful, how could I ensure I was being objective?

During the period that the intervention took place, there were number of students that left (two) and arrived (one) in the class. The final questionnaire was also completed during the last week of the school year, when a number of students had already left for the summer break. The number of students that completed each questionnaire was therefore different (first questionnaire – 21 students, second questionnaire – 16 students). Both the factors would have had an effect on the results, however the data still shows a significant change in the students' attitude towards discussions and spoken language.

To further validate my findings I would have liked to have collected data from a control group. Asking another class to complete questionnaires would have allowed me to make accurate comparisons between a class using artwork during discussions and another which did not.

As a result of the research I have been able to further develop my teaching and support the class more effectively. I have thought and reflected carefully on how to support my students to make progress in their spoken English and discussion skills. The majority of the class responded positively to the intervention – the children I wished it to have the most impact on developed and continue to develop their discussion skills week on week.

I hope I will be able to demonstrate the impact of using the arts as a tool across the curriculum. This is something that I and many others do as teachers, but doing this research will add extra weight to the beliefs I already have – that the arts are a powerful tool to motivate and develop a wide range of skills in children.

Next steps

This year the school has identified research as a key area to explore and develop. Staff will be carrying out action research projects over the coming months and years. My experience during this project puts me in a good position to support and work together with the school in this area.

I also hope to develop the use of artwork as a stimulus in the classroom, from using reproductions to using original pieces. Approaching artists and galleries to work with the school would provide students with the experience of viewing and interacting with real sculptures and other forms of art. The richness of discussion whilst looking at an original artwork would hopefully continue to develop the school aim of improved confidence in the spoken language of our students.

Greenvale School
Action research on the impact of music workshops for students with complex needs

Elizabeth Smith

Focus area and background

This action research project investigated the impact of music workshops at Greenvale School, a special needs school for students with learning difficulties, with a focus on students' communication, interaction and concentration skills.

Greenvale School is a community secondary special school for students between the ages of 11 and 19 years who have severe and profound learning difficulties including those with an additional diagnosis of autism. Many students also have additional physical and sensory disabilities. Class sizes vary between 6–12 students, with one teacher and two or three support assistants per class. There are 13 classes, with four classes that are 'High Needs' for students with more complex needs. These students typically work in a class of six students and four adults, and require a high level of support throughout the day. Students generally do not access specialist teaching rooms as they find transition around the school difficult, and have one teacher and regular support staff throughout the week. Students have their own outside space, and classrooms are generally sparse and distraction free with individual workstations.

The project involved five weeks of workshops for three High Needs classes led by Music Off Canvas, an organisation that provides interactive, improvised workshops. The workshops lasted for 45 minutes, and were led by two musicians from Music Off Canvas, supported by the class teacher and support staff. The research project focussed on one class, Class J, comprising of six students (Students 1–6) aged 14–19 and four staff. Of these six students two of the students are verbal with the other four communicating using gesture, symbols and vocalisations. Four students have autism. Ability ranges are between pre-national curriculum P2ii - P8.

Aims and rationale

The aims of the workshops were to provide students with opportunities to access music enrichment, and to develop their communication, interaction and concentration skills. As students in High Needs classes need a very structured environment, any enrichment opportunities they encounter are school based. Of the six students in Class J, two attend weekly music sessions in the school hall, however none of the students are able to access off site music enrichment for example concerts or workshops. It was hoped that through music enrichment students would develop their communication, interaction and concentration skills, for example being able to sit and participate in a group (music) activity for longer periods of time over the course of the workshops, to use communication through musical activities, and to focus on the instruments and workshop leaders.

Music was chosen as an enrichment activity as music is accessible to all, and does not rely on verbal language to communicate – it is an expressive arts form that everyone can access. Furthermore, there has been extensive research to show the benefits of music for students with special educational needs, for example musical and communication gains made by individuals with special needs who attended Gamelan workshops (MacDonald and Miell, 2000, p64), and through therapy, music can 'improve social behaviours, increase *focus and attention, increase communication attempts (vocalizations, verbalizations, gestures, and vocabulary), reduce anxiety, and improve body awareness and coordination'* (Journal of Music Therapy, 2004, p96). A further benefit to these workshops would be to develop the creative skills of the class team through participating in musical activities and enhancing their own creative expression (Macpherson and Bleasedale, 2012, p531).

Methodology

A questionnaire was conducted with the class team prior to the workshops taking place using both open and closed questions. These questions included using a Likert scale to rate students' engagement and participation in the maths lesson that would usually take place at the time of the music workshops. Originally, the questionnaire was about general engagement, however the maths lesson was chosen as this was the same time and day as the music workshops were scheduled, with the same teacher present. A similar questionnaire was repeated at the end of the workshops, with questions relating to engagement during music activities, communication and enjoyment of the arts. Short videos and photographs were taken throughout the workshops. Observation notes were taken at the end of each session, and comments notated from staff. An evaluation was sought from the workshop leaders at the end of the sessions. Ethics were taken into consideration and appropriate permission obtained from parents/carers and school staff.

Each music workshop followed a similar structure, and was led by two workshop leaders, however these were not always the same people each week. A hello song was sung to each student each week which included using the students name, and signs. The class then went on a journey around the world, using a train linking song with actions. As the students arrived at each country, different music was played with opportunities for students to participate by singing and/or signing and playing instruments. Workshop leaders would then demonstrate their instruments and various musical concepts, for example high/low before playing a variety of short extracts for students to listen to. A class goodbye song finished the session.

Results and Impact

The initial questionnaire showed all students engaged just as well if not better during the music workshops rather than the regular maths lesson, and that they were able to participate in the group music activities for the same or longer periods of time. For each student 'engagement' and 'participation' was very much a personal concept, for example for Student 3 this means responding to adult instructions and using key words to answer questions; for Student 6 it means sitting with adult support which involves hand massage and holding tactile objects to keep calm and focussed.

As all six students are very different and have individual strengths and needs, it is important to evaluate the progress each student has made during the music workshops. It is also important to note than many more external factors will influence the outcomes of this projects for example, changes in routines, new faces, quality of sleep the night before, or medication.

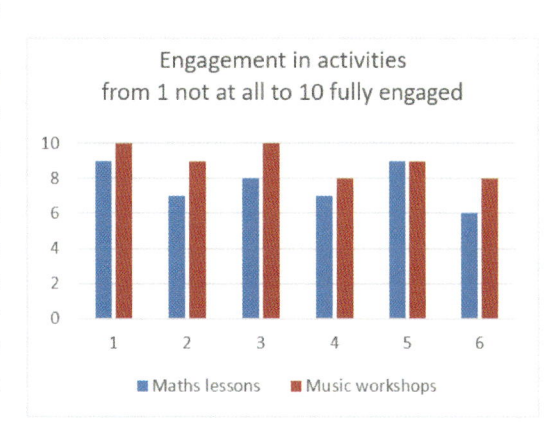

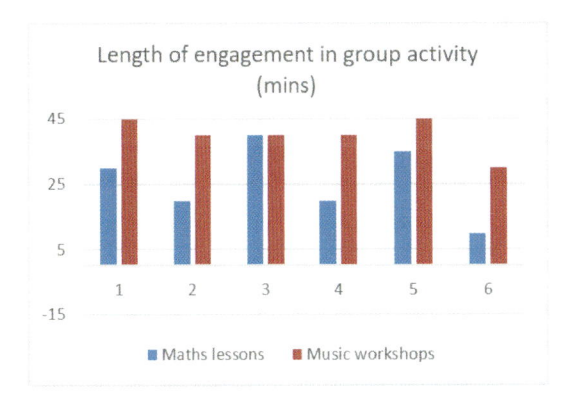

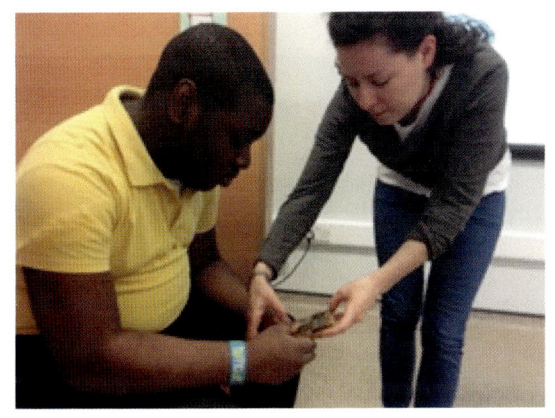

Length of engagement in group activity (mins)

[Bar chart comparing Maths lessons and Music workshops across 6 students]

From the beginning, Student 1 showed an enormous interest in the music workshops, and appeared much more engaged during music activities than maths activities. For example, Student 1 was very proactive and keen to play all the instruments offered, often reaching out to request a turn. During week one he reached out and felt the vibrations of the bassoon, repeating this activity during week two, and was described by staff after the session as *'very happy throughout, smiling and engaged'*. During the final week, he was able to play instruments with the workshop leaders in time, following their lead to start and stop. During maths lessons Student 1 would occasionally need to have time away from the group if he was unsettled, however he was able to stay focussed in the circle for the duration of every workshop, only moving away from the group to tidy up if instruments were left out.

Student 2 sat with a member of staff and was able to follow simple instructions to engage in the activities for example copying simple actions. He communicated clearly during the sessions, for example signing 'please' by touching his hand to his mouth when offered an instrument. Student 2 showed enjoyment when listening to the live music by rocking and clapping. He would need frequent movement breaks throughout the maths lessons, however was able to remain part of the group during the last music workshop.

Student 3 was interested in the workshops and engaged throughout the majority of them, however there were periods when due to night seizures he was sleepy and found it difficult to engage. Student 3 was able to engage in music activities, for example by saying key words during the hello and goodbye songs, and laughing at the high and low sounds the instruments made.

Student 4 sat with a member of staff next to him for all the music workshops. During maths lessons, he would frequently jump up and need to move around the room, however during week five he only moved away from the group once. As the workshops progressed, he was able to make eye contact with the workshop leaders, and take instruments from them although he was often a little reluctant to pass them back. When listening to the live music Student 4 was very calm and rocked to show his enjoyment.

Student 5 is always interested when visitors come to the classroom. She was able to communicate verbally with the workshop leaders, and learnt the names of instruments and different countries the music was from. In particular by the end of the sessions Student 5 was able to sing and sign the hello and goodbye songs, smiling and showing enjoyment when it was her turn. Student 5's behaviour was excellent during these sessions, a massive improvement on some maths lessons when she would frequently need support form a learning mentor to make good choices.

During week one, Student 6 did not participate in any of the activities and was either in the quiet room adjoining the classroom, or sat at the back of the classroom, however by week five she was able to sit with an adult in the circle and engage briefly in activities. This involved touching the mbira and shaking a tambourine, taking an instrument from an adult and passing it back once finished (rather than discarding it), and vocalising to show enjoyment of being sung to during the hello song.

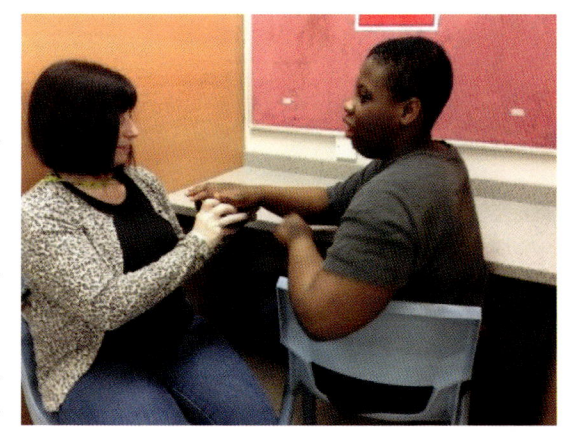

The workshop leaders saw improvements in the focus of the students, and some weeks *'the students were focussed almost entirely throughout the session'*, although they did note that if one student was not on task this then had an impact on others. As students became familiar with the workshop routines, they were able to participate more fully, in particular *'one student was able to sing the tune to the train song before we began'*. In the final week, they found students could answer simple questions on the instruments, and used more eye contact than previously, as well as showing a greater sense of interest and involvement.

Evaluation and conclusions

The music workshops had a positive impact on all students, with some students significantly benefitting more than others, for example Student 1. Although it is hard to generalise, all the students showed improvements in their communication throughout the sessions, with particular regard to making more eye contact, and learning key words/ signs during the regular songs. In particular, one student became very proactive with their communication to request instruments and activities. All the students coped well with the change in routine and meeting new staff, using symbol support to explain the change. By the end of the sessions, the students could all accept and engage in the exploration of instruments with the workshop leaders, and engaged with class staff as well. The concentration skills and engagement of the students also improved, both as a class and individually, with students remaining focussed in the group for the majority of each session. Class staff also reported more confidence in supporting and leading musical activities, and in subsequent weeks were able to adopt some of the practises learnt for example using the hello song during class music lessons.

The research process has been a fascinating opportunity to reflect and learn about the impact of music workshops. To improve further, it would have been better if students had individual aims to achieve throughout the workshops, as it has been hard to draw generalised conclusions from whole class aims due to small numbers and the variety of abilities and needs. It would also be useful to use more symbol and picture support during sessions, to aid students' communication further. There are many other factors that affect a students' communication, interaction and concentration, for example whether their bus was late to school, or if they have had a recent seizure, and further research would be needed to analyse the impact of these external factors. Reducing the workshop length to 30 minutes per session could also aid students' concentration throughout the sessions, and creating opportunities for staff and workshop leaders to meet prior to the sessions would enable a shared process for the workshops. If workshop leaders remained the same throughout the sessions, a greater consistency across the workshops could then be achieved, building upon the strengths from the previous weeks and developing stronger relationships.

Next steps

It is hoped in the next academic year that the relationship with Music Off Canvass will continue. A revision to the model will be considered, for example arranging pre-workshop visits and meetings, joint planning, and team-teaching some sessions, which will also further develop the class teachers' skills. A pre-visit and meeting is a similar model to that used by The Royal Academy of Arts who arranged a pre-visit to a Year 7 class for the afternoon, meeting with the class teacher and observing the students, prior to a day visit to the art gallery. Mousetrap Theatre also offer bespoke workshops for SEN groups, however both of these are fully funded or heavily discounted, therefore applying for a funding bid for a future music project would significantly impact on the ability to develop the relationship further for both staff and students. During further workshops, communication and interaction skills can be further developed by planning paired musical activities with the students; opportunities for students to make choices, for example which instruments to play, which country the train stops at; and opportunities for students to lead by starting and stopping the music or changing the speed.

References

Grayson, H. and Howells, V. (2016) Music Off Canvass evaluation.

MacDonald, R. and Miell, D. (2000) Creativity and Music Education: The Impact of Social Variables, in *International Journal of Music Education November 2000 vol. os-36 no. 1 58–68*.

Available at: http://ijm.sagepub.com/content/os-36/1/58.full.pdf+html [Accessed August 2016].

Macpherson, H.M. and Bleasedale, B. (2012) 'Journeys in ink: Re-presenting the spaces of inclusive arts practice', *Cultural Geographies, 19(4)*: 523–534.

Smith, E. (2016) Workshop log and notes, Greenvale School.

Whipple, J. (2004) Music in intervention for children and adolescents with autism: a meta-analysis' in *Journal for Music Therapy, Summer; 41(2)*:90–106.

Available at: http://www.ncbi.nlm.nih.gov/pubmed/15307805

[Accessed August 2016].

Website links

http://www.greenvale.lewisham.sch.uk/Latest-News

http://www.mousetrap.org.uk/index.php/special-educational-needs/theatre-offers-for-special-school-groups.html

http://www.musicoffcanvas.com/special-needs-workshops.html

https://www.royalacademy.org.uk/teachers-and-students-2

QEII Jubilee School
How can creative arts support the engagement of hard to reach young people?
Paul Morrow

Creative Practice and Wellbeing are both wide ranging topics with the potential for many areas of research. We decided to narrow the focus and adopt a systematic approach in an effort to understand whether, for some young people, engagement as a measure of wellbeing was increased by activities offered within the art room.

What is creative practice?
When looking at the research project one of the first things we wanted to do was to think about our practice. The reason for this is that as an SEN practitioner our approach can be quite different from that of our mainstream colleagues. We wanted to be clear that when we described engagement that this was engagement that could be seen within a creative activity and supported by creative practice.

Context
At QEII Jubilee School we meet the needs of a wide range of young people with complex barriers to learning such as PMLD (profound and multiple learning difficulties), SLD (severe learning difficulties), complex ASD (autistic spectrum disorder) and rare syndromes. It is important to note here that these acronyms signpost the potential difficulties these young people experience but do not define them or their potential.

Within our population some of these young people can be considered hard to reach; by this I mean young people that have significant developmental delay, usually co-morbid with other conditions that can inhibit learning. These young people might be non-verbal, they may use limited signs or no signs at all. The young people may gesture towards needs and wants or indicate via eye gaze. As a consequence of this we use a range of pedagogical approaches to reach students in order to deliver a meaningful and appropriate curriculum.

Why explore this area?

We chose to examine this area for a number of reasons. We have for a period of time now seen the potential of the creative arts to support wellbeing. Approaches within both art and music have been informed by art and music therapy. The approach is one that supports expression, engagement and autonomy.

There has been a greater focus on the issue of mental health and wellbeing within education for a period of time now and within the SEN population there is an increased propensity towards developing mental health and wellbeing issues. There can also be a disjuncture within education settings where academic education can be seen as separate from those interventions that are specifically designed to support wellbeing, such as therapies and mentoring. There was an opportunity here explore how education, specifically a creative and cultural education can by its characteristics support a young person's wellbeing.

Wellbeing and engagement; a connection

During the international conference on wellbeing held at the Royal Society in November 2003, the opening address described *'Wellbeing as any positive and sustainable state of mind which allows individuals and nations to thrive and flourish'* (Bailey, 2012:4).

Martin Seligman (2011) stresses the role of engagement in supporting emotional wellbeing; he places engagement as a core component of wellbeing that merges both cognitive and emotional resources. The interrelatedness of well being and engagement is described as 'flow' by Martin Seligman; *'I* believe that the concentrated attention that flow requires uses up all the cognitive and emotional resources that make up thought and feeling.' During the flow we merge with the object. This supports our position that we believe that when our students are engaged that they are in flow and that we are supporting their wellbeing needs. *'I believe that the concentrated attention that flow requires uses up all the cognitive and emotional resources that make up thought and feeling.'*

Signifiers of creative practice

We decided to describe the signifiers of creative practice so we could identify an activity that had these characteristics. We had the opportunity to share these findings at the Royal Academy of Arts SEN (special educational needs) and creativity conference; Why and How 2016. This was a great catalyst to explore this area in a deeper fashion.

Exploring characteristics of creative practice within the art room

The approach within the art room sits within an inclusive education model; learning is opportunity based, the potential for leaning is not limited as there is no predetermined outcome or limitation and value is based on process. Learning is anticipated and an appropriate and meaningful curriculum is developed and this is often multi-sensory in nature.

Multi-sensory teaching and creative practice; how do they fit?

This approach can also securely sit within contemporary art practice:

- It has elements of experience and perception; the subjective.
- It has elements of improvisation, performance, participation; meaning is constructed and generated by the participant.

- It is located within a postmodern paradigm; many narratives and multiple entry points and can be viewed as inclusive and democratic.
- All these elements place multi-sensory teaching within the realms of contemporary art practice.

(Modified from the presentation by Michelle Lee and Paul Anderson, *Curriculum, Art and Multi-Sensory Experiences: How Does It All Fit Together?*, at the *Why and How?* conference March 2016 at The Royal Academy of Arts)

Engagement as a measure of wellbeing

Wellbeing is hard to define as constituent parts are wide and varied and it's seen as being multi-dimensional and influenced by a wide range of socioeconomic factors. For this reason we have chosen to focus on one measurable and tangible characteristic; engagement. We believe that a young person can only engage and attend to a task if that young person's wellbeing is being met through the task in which they are engaged.

So we believe that when a young person is intrinsically motivated and engages with an activity of a creative characteristic that this activity is supporting that young person's wellbeing.

How to measure wellbeing; developing a tool

Initially we adopted a grounded theory approach. However this proved difficult within the time constraints of the project. We wanted this research project to help us to move forward with a qualitative tool that would allow us to assess and give insights on how to support individual development.

As part of the school's continual professional development Professor Barry Carpenter had delivered training on the engagement profile and its use and implication within SEN teaching. The acting Head of School had championed this approach and saw the potential relationship between engagement and wellbeing.

The engagement profile and the Creative Arts supporting hard to reach young people

Engagement profile what is it?

> Engagement is the single best predictor of successful learning for children with learning disabilities. (Iovannone et al., 2003), Without engagement, there is no deep learning (Hargreaves, 2006), effective teaching, meaningful outcome, real attainment or quality progress. (Carpenter, 2010).
>
> (ComplexId.ssatrust.org.uk, 2016)

As engagement is multifaceted and encompasses a number of characteristics the engagement profile defines these as:

- Awareness
- Curiosity
- Investigation
- Discovery
- Anticipation
- Persistence
- Initiation.

By using these headings a clear picture is drawn up that describes when and how these students are most engaged. These headings then allow for interventions to be designed that can increase a young person's engagement. These interventions are recorded and their effectiveness graded, this then creates a picture of potential next steps.

The story

There were a number of factors present here that needed to be unpicked to ensure that the approach was sustainable. Part of our question was unpacking pre-existing practice so that we could have signifiers that would define cultural and creative practice within our locale. This would enable us to develop a shared language and understanding of these terms. After this we used the engagement profile to explore student engagement during these activities. We characterised the young person's engagement using the descriptors supplied by the engagement profile. This indicated when the young person was most engaged; this then defined how we could then potentially extend and support the young person's engagement.

Planning and implementation of the intervention

The vast majority of the project timeline was the research that preceded the intervention, this ensured that we had a sound base from which to proceed. However due to the day to day pressures we had to modify the proposed timeline so that we had an achievable outcome. One of the most time consuming but useful and rewarding aspects of the intervention was the examination of the pedagogy that was used within the art room. Here we had to unpick this and consider this not only within an education model but also within contemporary art practice. We presented these findings at the Royal Academy of Art's conference on creativity and SEN to our peers, not only teachers, but also artists and gallery and museum professionals. Here we looked at a specific instance and by applying descriptors of both contemporary art practice and inclusive education we located the pedagogy within both paradigms. The rigorous processes of articulating this to our peers helped us to feel confident in the language that we developed.

The next stage was problematic; initially we had used the engagement profile with three hard to reach young people. However as time progressed it became evident that it would be difficult to design a number of interventions based on the information garnered. To have a more meaningful experience we focused on one student within the upper school, I will refer to him as student A.

Results and impact

Piloting

As mentioned previously, we initially developed profiles of three hard to reach students who were considered to engage more within the art room. One of the many benefits was joint working; the exercise itself brought a range of people together to share their knowledge of the young people and to describe when they were most engaged. We then moved to examining one specific student in greater detail; student A.

Student A is a looked after student, he is non-verbal and has a range of learning needs. After initially profiling the characteristics of when student A was most engaged, we then translated one of these characteristics to a part of their school day when they are recorded as being less engaged.

The outcomes of the intervention proved useful in two ways; firstly there was a 'tool kit' that could be referenced when student A was less engaged so that a level of contingency was available throughout the lesson. There was also a discernible impact on the student's level of engagement, however sometimes this wasn't consistent. Due to the nature of the tool, the process supported reflection and indicated changes that might increase engagement. The project itself enabled the school to pull together a number of factors such as mental health, wellbeing and creative and cultural practice.

Evaluation

There were some issues in regard to timings. The first stage of the research – defining characteristics of practice were explored in a meaningful and robust manner. However the later parts of the research, namely the piloting were more problematic. The research process had to be adapted to overcome issues of time constraints. Schools and teachers are time poor; trying to find time to meaningfully engage and undertake research was difficult in itself. The research process had to be refined so that it would give the information we needed to inform the next steps. There was also the tension of developing a school wide movement within these constraints. It might suggest here that what we were looking at was too complex to achieve within this time frame but the information that was garnered puts the school in a strong position to move forward.

Next steps

We now have a strong position from which to progress. We have successfully defined the characteristics of creative and cultural pedagogy within QEII Jubilee School that affirms our practice. We have a tool that now articulates engagement and informs next steps to increase a young person's engagement when participating in these activities. And we feel that we have demonstrated a potential link between engagement and wellbeing for young people with SEN.

Our next steps are to use this knowledge and embed this further across the school as one of the tools that can support teaching. We also now have a starting point to from which to begin a conversation to expand our understanding of wellbeing and how we can measure this within a hard to reach population of young people with SEN. We are currently working with Creative Futures who are using the engagement profile in a pilot project with us.

References

Bailey, G (2012) *Emotional Wellbeing for Children with Special Educational Needs and Disabilities*. London. Sage

Seligman, MEP (2011) *Flourish: A New Understanding of Happiness and Wellbeing and How to Achieve Them*. London. Nicholas Brearley

Authentichappiness.sas.upenn.edu. (2016). *What is Well-Being? | Authentic Happiness*. [online] Available at: https://www.authentichappiness.sas.upenn.edu/learn/wellbeing [Accessed September 2016].

Complexld.ssatrust.org.uk. (2016). *SSATrust – Engagement profile & scale*. [online] Available at: http://complexld.ssatrust.org.uk/project-resources/engagement-profile-scale.html [Accessed September 2016].

Website links

https://www.authentichappiness.sas.upenn.edu/learn/wellbeing

http://complexld.ssatrust.org.uk/project-resources/engagement-profile-scale.htm

ARTS AWARD AND ITS IMPACT
Lansbury Lawrence Community School
Can art help children raise attainment in reading?

Kerri Sellens

This report details an art based action research project conducted at Lansbury Lawrence primary school in Poplar, within the London borough of Tower Hamlets. The aim of the project was to see if art could provide an opportunity for developing readers to engage further with books and reading. The inspiration for the project came from one of the school development plan priorities for 2015–2016; to raise attainment in reading across the school. As the school's specialist art teacher, I was interested in whether I could use my specialism to help raise attainment in another subject.

Lansbury Lawrence is a two form entry community school, with 94% of the children deriving from Minority Ethnic Groups, and 87% classed as having English as an Additional Language. From the school's 2015 KS2 SATs there was a dip in the reading results, with progress also slightly below the national median, this data led to the school development plan focus on reading for the following year.

The research project began in January 2016, working with a group of 12 children aged between 8–11 years. Children were selected to take part through discussion with class teachers, phase leaders and the head teacher. Children who were currently reading at a level below their expected age range were chosen. From baseline assessment data, on average, the cohort was reading at a level two years below their actual age.

To work regularly with children from different year groups at the same time was a logistical challenge, so the project was organised as a weekly after school club. As I also wanted to introduce Arts Award provision within our school, I decided to use the Arts Award Explore framework to provide additional structure and focus to the project.

At first some of the children were reluctant to attend, and one set of parents was hesitant to send them. This was due to the children not having a particular interest in art, and the parents thinking it was not an important enough extracurricular subject to study over maths or English. Reassurance that the project had a focus on a core subject through art convinced the parents that the after school club would be worthwhile, and the goal of achieving an Arts Award qualification inspired the children to give it a go.

During the first session, the children completed a questionnaire about their attitudes towards both art and reading. Questions included:

Do you enjoy reading? Why?

Only two children answered no; one writing because it was boring, and the other saying it was tiring. Two children answered that reading was OK, and that they liked it a little bit.

'It's OK because you learn words.'

The last eight children all answered yes they enjoyed reading. Reasons why included because it was fun and also, as with other children's answers, because of the vocabulary.

'I enjoy reading because you find interesting words and when they get to an exciting part I keep reading on.'

Do you think making art could help you with your reading? Why?

From the 12 children surveyed, five answered no because they thought they were separate subjects with no similarities. The remaining seven children answered yes, although they weren't really sure why.

'I think so but I am not sure really.'

'So it helps me copy the front of the book picture.'

After some initial drawing exercises to help the group get to know each other and work comfortably together, the project began with reading The Child who was Wild by Michael Rosen:

The Child Who Was Wild

Once there was a woman, a young, young woman
She ran from the city, the old, old city
She ran to the woods, the deep dark woods

She wasn't seen for days. Days, weeks and months.
She came out of the woods, the deep dark woods
She came with a child, a child who was wild.

She brought the child to the city, the old, old city
He grew and he grew and he grew and he grew
Out of his hands grew shoots: green shoots and leaves
Out of his shoulders grew the lily and the rose
His hair was the blossom that blows in the wind,
He stood in the city, the old, old city
with the leaves and the flowers and the blossom
falling, falling, falling on grey, grey gravel.

(Michaelrosen.co.uk, 2016)

The children were asked to imagine and talk about the different characters and settings within the poem. The responses were literal, with descriptions of a boy and a woman, a built up city and a wood full of trees. They then went on to draw what they had described. With the poem printed on to acetate and overlaid on the drawing, the words could be read again with the illustrations drawn by the children given equal importance. Over the next few weeks we carried on exploring the same poem through printmaking and sculpture, focussing on character and setting. The children became confident with the content of the poem, and two children brought in drawings with the poem written out that they had made at home independently.

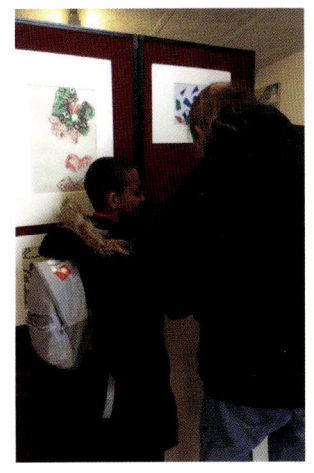

As part of the project, and to show how art could be made and interpreted in different ways, the group visited the nearby Nunnery Gallery and saw an exhibition of photographs by Mariele Neudecker.

During another session, an artist who specialises in horticultural work, Kirsti Davies, worked with the group explaining her thought process and art techniques.

The project progressed to children interpreting favourite books that they had read. Not all of the group had a favourite book, so we used the school library to help find books that would hold interest. Using the art skills developed over the preceding weeks, the children then made their own decisions as to how to visualise their chosen text. Again, the interpretations of the text were literal, focussing mostly on character description. When asked what their work was based on, and why they were making it, all children could answer with the name of the book and a brief summary of what the story was about. Visualising thoughts and feelings on the text were harder concepts for the group to translate.

The enthusiasm for the project within the group was now very evident. The commitment was overwhelming, with all of the children giving up an hour of their time each week after school and even asking to work on their projects during lunchtimes. It was a highlight of the project to see this engagement progress and develop.

The project culminated with an exhibition for the children's families showcasing their finished art work in May 2016. Every member of the group explained to their families what they had made, and the book they had based their work upon.

Amongst the tangible outcomes of the project the children all demonstrated raised self-esteem and confidence within both art and reading. All of the children also passed their Arts Award Explore accredited qualifications. Watching the children receive their certificates in the whole school achievement assembly was fantastic. One parent, whose son is about to go to secondary school, told me that he was now going to continue with art as a GCSE option.

The children were reassessed by their teachers, to see if there had been an improvement in their reading levels. Two of the children were assessed at a reading level below that which they started on, while all of the other children improved in reading age between 1–25 months. Two of the children were assessed as reading at a level above their expected age range.

Any progress made cannot be totally credited to the research project, as there were other lessons and interventions taking place at the same time, such as daily guided reading within each class. And of course, children cannot be conclusively defined by their capacity to perform in tests. However, from a final questionnaire given to the children some interesting data was collected.

Did you enjoy the link with reading? Did it change the way you feel about reading at all?

'I did and it changed my feeling towards reading.'

'Now I like reading thanks to my club and I feel happy.'

Do you think making art could help you with your reading? Why?

All of the children answered yes, with answers including;

'Yes because if you get inspired then you are really eager to read.'

'Yes because it helped me understand the stories that we did.'

'If you read a book you can imagine an image in your head.'

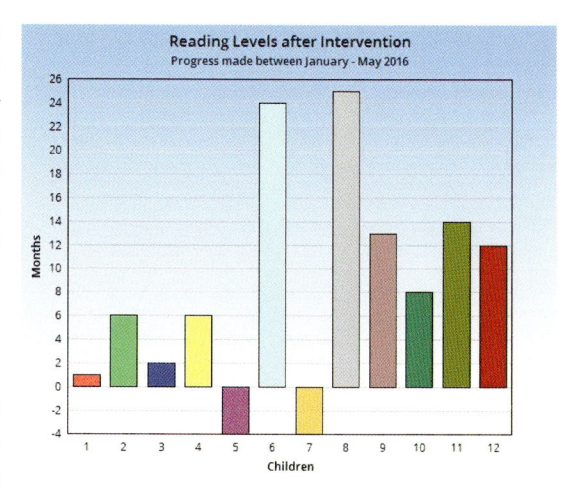

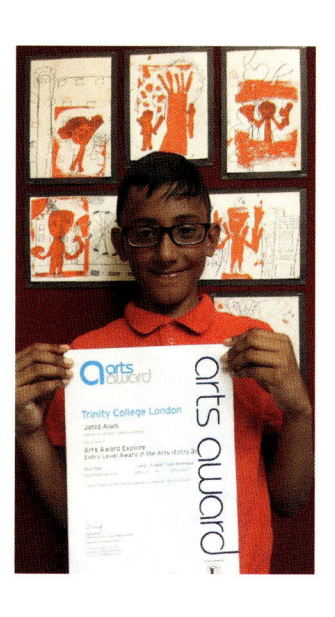

Connections had been made within the children's different areas of learning; and art for these children had helped to develop understanding within reading. From the four children within the cohort who took their Year 6 SATs shortly afterwards, three of them met the expected standard within their reading paper.

I really enjoyed the research process, and discovering new ways of seeing and making alongside the children. Arts Award is now firmly embedded within our school, with children asking if they can be a part of the next group of children to take part. I do feel this model of research and teaching would be transferable to any school setting, and is a worthwhile exercise to potentially engage children in a way that suits their particular learning style.

If I were to run the same project again, I would have a comparable group of children outside of the intervention, against which to monitor and measure the progress made. It would have been interesting to compare different groups of children. However, witnessing the sense of pride and achievement the children had when presenting their work and ideas to their parents made the project more than worthwhile and successful.

References

Michaelrosen.co.uk. (2016). ::: *Michael Rosen – The Website* :::. [online] Available at: http://www.michaelrosen.co.uk/once.html [Accessed September 2016].

Chingford Academies Trust
Encouraging participation, learning and achievement in the arts through interaction with Arts Award, working with young people in receipt of Pupil Premium funding

Yolanda Guns

This innovative, bespoke project was created to help young people gain an understanding of the artists who lived in their local area from whom they could gain inspiration, as well as the opportunity to become familiar with the cultural landscape within their locality.

Focus area

We decided to focus on sharing our expertise in Arts Award delivery by creating a new programme which would allow students in receipt of Pupil Premium funding to find out more about the cultural opportunities on offer within their 'home' borough of Waltham Forest and engage and interact with the arts and cultural sector.

Aims

Our aims were to:

- Recruit groups of pupils from local primary schools, concentrating on those in receipt of Pupil Premium funding, with whom we could deliver a bespoke Waltham Forest focussed Discover Arts Award programme in collaboration with our own Arts Award students from

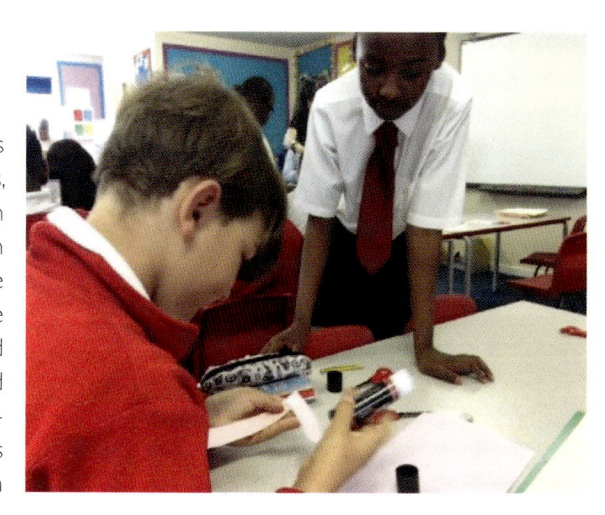

Chingford Foundation School, who were working toward their Bronze or Silver Arts Award qualifications.
- Create an awareness and understanding of the benefits of engaging with Arts Award in primary schools who had not been involved previously, via a project with a 'local' arts focus. We also wanted to ensure that our partner primary schools had positive learning experiences and that the pupils achieved their 'Discover' Arts Award.
- Prepare bespoke 'Discover' materials for the pupils to accompany their learning journey through the three sections of the 'Discover' award and also design appropriate resources to accompany our Chingford Foundation School students as part of their Bronze and Silver Arts Award journey.
- Use Arts Award students from Chingford Foundation School to help deliver some of the practical activities to primary school groups as part of their own Arts Award activities and to act as positive role models and CFS Arts Award Ambassadors for this purpose.
- Ensure that all those involved in the project learned about the rich cultural offer available within Waltham Forest.
- Engender the sustainability of a Waltham Forest centred Arts Award programme for KS2 and KS3 students, to encourage students and their families to interact with a range of local arts initiatives and arts centres.

Rationale

Waltham Forest is an arts-rich borough with an amazing cultural heritage. It houses both William Morris Gallery (the former home of William Morris) and Vestry House Museum, which provides a local history viewpoint with an ever-changing range of exhibitions. There are also arts centres and collectives of local professional arts practitioners. In addition, there are notable local artists, who have been made 'peers of the realm' in recognition of their contribution to the world of the arts, such as Sir Alfred Hitchcock and, more recently, Sir Matthew Bourne, in recognition of his services to dance. Such influential figures should help provide our young people with aspirations to follow a career path in the arts industries and, through their work as part of Arts Award, to discover how these careers might be accessed.

It had become apparent however through research conducted by the institutions, that many sectors of local Waltham Forest residents have no interaction with either William Morris Gallery or Vestry House Museum and seem to be unaware of the contribution that engagement with cultural institutions can bring in terms of developing an understanding of arts and culture within families. The students in receipt of Pupil Premium funding are those statistically least likely to interact with local arts and culture and many of these young people have families who have relocated to the area and have no previous knowledge of its cultural heritage. For all of the students chosen to become involved with our action based research project, none of them had previously visited William Morris Gallery or Vestry House Museum or participated in any of the community learning opportunities which had been offered. Through our project, we hoped to address these issues alongside our aim to show how interaction with Arts Award can benefit young people and enthuse them through arts-related learning.

Background context

Chingford Foundation School is a large co-educational comprehensive school in Chingford, North East London. Originally built in the 1930's, it has continued to change and develop over the decades into the over-subscribed and highly successful community school and sixth form that we see today. In 2008, Chingford Foundation School was awarded Specialist School status in Arts and Humanities. This was also the year when the school first registered as an Arts Award centre and held its first moderation.

In 2009, the school became an Arts Award Supporter Centre and was able to extend its Arts Award offer to all those young people who could access this fully inclusive, extracurricular programme. From this point onwards, Chingford Foundation School entered an amazing period of growth and development in the arts. The school achieved an Artsmark Silver award in 2010, followed by an Artsmark Gold award in 2013 and was then selected as an Artsmark Good Practice Centre in 2014/15. This success has been replicated and surpassed in terms of Arts Award. Since 2008, the school has held 22 moderations with a 100% success rate. Students have been entered for Bronze, Silver and Gold Arts Awards during this time, including Shakespeare Challenge and the Special Edition projects such as 'London 2012' and now the 'WW1' specification. Chingford Foundation School became the first school in London to enter students for their Gold Arts Award and in 2014 also became the first London school to enter young people for their 'WW1' Arts Awards. The Arts Award students have been featured in a number of national case studies on the Arts Award website, and in a variety of publications through ENYAN and Creative Pages. The Arts Award programme is known across the local community with regular events being held at the local South Chingford Community Library, in various churches and at community fetes such as Chingford Village Festival. The local MP, Iain Duncan Smith has visited the Arts Award cohort on a number of occasions to learn more about the work being carried out and to present certificates.

In September 2012, Chingford Foundation School became the founder member of Chingford Academies Trust and was joined by Rushcroft Foundation School. Within a few weeks of this partnership being established, Arts Award was offered to the students from both schools and activities and events organised by the Arts Co-ordinator for the Trust, have been available to young people in both establishments.

In 2016, our students were selected to form the 'focus group' to work with the Marketing Manager at Arts Award to contribute ideas toward the Arts Award Week to celebrate the 10th birthday of the scheme, and Chingford Foundation School was also given the opportunity to run a workshop as part of the Gold Expo event held at Rich Mix at the end of June. A further highlight of the year was the acknowledgement of the school's prowess in Arts Award delivery through being selected as an Arts Award Good Practice Centre 2015/16.

The story

We remained true to our vision of creating and delivering arts programmes which allowed the young people from our Pupil Premium cohorts at Chingford Academies Trust and at our partner primary schools, to develop new art form knowledge and understanding, and learn through a student-centred, creative approach. We devised programmes to look at arts and culture in Waltham Forest and also to look at iconic figures with a specific link to the area. As we were delivering both a combined arts programme and a WW1 Special Edition Arts Award programme for the young people, we also introduced the stories of local WW1 heroes to our pupil cohort which enabled the learning of historical information delivered through an arts-led approach. We worked with groups of pupils from five primary schools, drawn from the North, Centre and South of the borough to deliver Discover Arts Award and with our own students from Chingford Academies Trust to deliver Bronze and Silver Arts Award projects.

My role

As Arts Co-ordinator for Chingford Academies Trust, I lead our Arts Award programme delivery and manage our various cross-arts projects. I led on this Arts Award Waltham Forest Arts and Culture Pupil-Premium initiative and took responsibility for:

- Devising this bespoke course including liaison with William Morris Gallery and Vestry House Museum.
- Writing the course booklet for students.
- Recruiting the primary schools to take part in the project.
- Organising the outreach learning sessions at William Morris Gallery and Vestry House Museum.
- Liaising with the link teachers in all of the primary schools.
- Delivering the initial meeting with parents to introduce the project.
- Co-delivering the various Arts Award sessions at the primary schools.
- Supporting our own Arts Award students from Chingford Academies Trust in using their work with primary school pupils to gather their evidence for their own Arts Award portfolios.
- Assessing all Discover, Bronze and Silver Arts Award portfolios in preparation for successful moderations.
- Organising certificate celebrations for the various student and school groups.

How we did it

The schools we worked with were very different from one another. Some had very formal learning arrangements and others adopted a more contemporary outlook with teachers being addressed by their first names. Some of the schools had a school uniform policy and others did not. In addition, some of the primary schools we worked with were already aware of both Artsmark and Arts Award and others had not yet considered engagement with either programme. All of our schools however were judged by Ofsted to be at least 'Good' or 'Outstanding'. One of our partner primary schools was part of an 'all through' school and another was a Primary Pupil Referral Unit.

In addition to the schools which form part of Chingford Academies Trust, we recruited our primary school partners for this action research project by addressing a meeting of local primary school Headteachers to talk about our project, and invited expressions of interest. Once we had arrived at a cohort of schools, we met with the teachers from each school who were going to be our 'link' staff for the duration of the project. This meeting in advance of the project implementation allowed us to get an understanding of the groups we were going to be working with and to discuss our shared goals. Each school had control over the group size, year groups selected and the student cohort. In addition to our project delivery, we offered each school the opportunity for us to host an initial meeting with parents to introduce Arts Award and explain about what their children would be doing. We also offered to mount an exhibition of the pupils' work at the project's conclusion. We worked with pupils from Year 3 right through to Year 6 at our primary schools during this project and with students between Years 7 and 9 from Chingford Academies Trust.

Our classroom delivery for our 'Discover' projects concentrated on teaching a Combined Arts programme, where learning was centred around creativity as the starting point and learners were encouraged to use their imagination to direct the pathway to their produced outcomes. We covered creative writing and poetry, art and craft work, drama, dance and song-writing across the participating schools. Our Chingford Academies Trust students, who accompanied us to deliver some of the sessions as part of their Arts Leadership activities for their Bronze Part D Arts Award or their Silver Unit 2 Arts Award 'taught' Drama, Streetdance, Craft, Design, Creative Writing and Poetry workshops.

As part of our Arts and Culture project, pupils were able to visit William Morris Gallery and Vestry House Museum and subsequently produced a number of presentations about William Morris and his work as well as lots of examples of art and craft based on his style and themes. They also learned about Alfred Hitchcock and his work and his contribution to the world of film, and this also generated a number of presentations and visual displays. Our KS3 Arts Award students extended this unit by also researching the life and work of Sir Matthew Bourne and his award for his contribution to the world of dance. Those students, from across both primary and secondary school settings who were participating in our WW1 Arts Award project learned about the local heroes who were decorated for their wartime contribution, and this provided an ideal starting point for both drama role-play and creative writing.

Results and impact

As a result of our work during this action research project, we have achieved the following:

- The creation of five new Arts Award centres in Waltham Forest.
- 146 pupils achieved an Arts Award Discover certificate with 28 pupils achieving a Special Edition WW1 Discover certificate.
- 17 students from Chingford Academies Trust achieved their Bronze (Level 1) Arts Award and nine students achieved their Silver (Level 2) Arts Award.
- Six of our KS3 students achieved their WW1 Special Edition Bronze (Level 1) Arts Award and a further two KS3 students achieved their Silver (Level 2) WW1 Special Edition Arts Award.
- All schools involved are now aware of Arts Award and its positive impact on the lives of the pupils who engage with it and will hopefully continue to be a part of our Waltham Forest Arts Award Community.

Chingford Academies Trust organises the Waltham Forest Arts Award Network, which hold meetings once a term during the academic year.

We wanted to use our expertise in the delivery of Arts Award as a vehicle for encouraging pupils in receipt of Pupil Premium to engage with arts opportunities and gain inspiration and knowledge about career pathways in the arts through finding out about iconic artists with a connection to their local area. We feel we have been successful in this mission.

Pupils and families from the cohort involved in our action research project are now aware of the art and cultural icons associated with Waltham Forest and have evidenced this through their Arts Award portfolios.

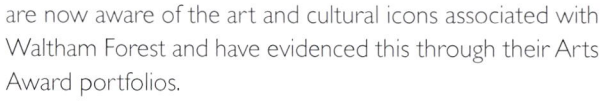

Pupils and families from the cohort involved in our project are now aware of the William Morris Gallery and Vestry House Museum and its community offer. Again, this is evidenced through Arts Award portfolios and the presentation given about this topic by Chingford Academies Trust's students at our last Arts Award Network Meeting, which was held in June at William Morris Gallery.

Schools involved have seen the learning, attendance and behavioural benefits provided by engaging with Arts Award. At all our schools, attendance was excellent throughout our project within our cohort. Pupils knew which days we were coming into school and looked forward to the sessions. They were even example of students being absent from school for medical appointments etc. and returning especially to attend our extracurricular timetabled sessions!

Behaviour was also consistently excellent, although we were aware that many of the students we were working with had behavioural issues generally. The pupils were enthused by the arts-focussed and personalised approach to learning which motivated them to stay on task. We noticed that retention of information was also excellent across the cohort. Students were able to retain facts and figures about the work they had done right through the project and on to moderation day itself where the Bronze and Silver students had to talk to the Moderator about their programmes. We also saw a gradual, on-going and rewarding increase in the self-confidence and self-esteem of the pupils involved. As the sessions progressed, more and more students became willing to share their ideas and work with their group. They also became ever more comfortable about working in a group environment with children they might not normally interact with during the school day.

Personal reflection on impact

When personally considering the impact of this project on myself, my colleague John Hunter, who co-delivered the school-based Arts Award sessions, our link teachers from the primary schools and other arts practitioners and educators, there is much to feel pleased about in terms of the positive impact on the lives of the young people involved. From my own point of view, I found the project both challenging and exciting. It was illuminating in particular to witness how students enjoyed learning about people who came from their local area and made highly successful careers in the arts. It was also thought-provoking and exciting in terms of the development of young arts leaders, to watch how proficient our students were in delivering their 'teaching' sessions and how they clearly role-modelled their own vision of good teaching. Of most significance I felt was that the whole concept of the inclusivity of Arts Award allowed all of our young people from such a variety of different settings to achieve their very best! Having set up five new Arts Award centres within the borough, it is to be hoped that their engagement with Arts Award will be on-going and they are aware that I will welcome them to become a part of our local Arts Award Area Network and provide any support they require.

There is a real place in education I feel, for young people to learn about local history and their local heroes. It allows them to develop their own dreams of success and become inspired by the local role models who prove that the impossible can be attainable!

Evaluation

The research process provided an ideal opportunity to test theories and ideas based on our feelings about the benefits of Arts Award on young people. It also allowed us to prioritise working with Pupil Premium groups of students and test our theory that this group was the least likely to engage with local arts institutions and activities. We feel satisfied that because of this project so many young people have gained certification which will be of benefit to them in the future alongside acquiring new skills and knowledge. Our students were overwhelmingly positive about their experience and the following evaluative comments demonstrate this.

> *This programme is all about creativity through free learning. It gives me a chance to share my talents as I develop them. It's a programme where you can decide what you want to do and it is your choice of how you do it and how far you want to take it. It offers opportunities which you would not normally get a chance to experience at school and has taught me a lot about researching people and places for my portfolio which otherwise I would never have found out about.*
>
> Year 8 student.

> *Where can I begin? This is a fantastic, amazing opportunity and experience to be a part of, with new challenges that push you to find out what you are capable of and then express these talents and share them with new people. I*

have learned Arts Leadership skills in teaching my lessons and also developed skills in creative writing through creating my WW1 letters for people to read and review. These two aspects are examples of things I was afraid to try at the beginning of my Silver and yet now have become things I really love to do.

Year 9 student

Our Bronze and Silver Arts Award moderation was held on 29th July 2016, at which our students involved in this project presented their portfolios and met with the Moderator to discuss their work. The Moderator commented: *'Some amazing projects which have fulfilled all areas of evidence and assessment criteria. The young people have had an amazing experience and have learned so much from this Arts Award opportunity.'*

Following this moderation a parent commented: *'My daughters have just come home and told me that they have both passed their moderations. Thank you for all your hard work and the motivation that you have provided them with. They are now looking forward to continuing on to the next level of Arts Award.'*

Next steps

This project met, and exceeded, my expectations in terms of positive outcomes. It has inspired me to explore ways in which I can build upon what I have introduced, in order to make this programme a sustainable course. Future generations of Pupil Premium students, as well as those from other target groups, such as More Able or ESOL cohorts, should be allowed the opportunity to gain skills and knowledge and use creative approaches to enhance learning outcomes. Alongside gaining an Arts Award qualification, the young people will also develop an understanding of the cultural background which defines the area in which they live. The first of the 'next steps' therefore, will be to explore ways of successfully funding this development of our action research project, in order for it to reach a wider audience.

Queensbridge Primary School
The impact of introducing the Discover Arts Award to Pupil Premium children in Year 2

Rhiannon Mapleston

Focus area

This case study looks at the impact of introducing the Discover Arts Award to Pupil Premium children in a Year 2 class in an inner city school in London.

Aims

This project aimed to give Pupil Premium children an extended opportunity to explore the arts, and raise the profile of the arts in their education by children identifying artists and art forms they had explored. It also aimed to develop Pupil Premium children's confidence in the arts.

Rationale

The Pupil Premium is additional funding for publicly funded schools in England to raise the attainment of disadvantaged pupils and close the gap between them and their peers.
Department for Education, 2016[12]

It is widely documented that statistically, disadvantaged children do not achieve as well as their peers.[13] The Pupil Premium funding is allocated to children who are currently

---

[12] Gov.uk. (2014). *Pupil premium: funding and accountability for schools – Detailed guidance – GOV.UK.* [online] Available at: https://www.gov.uk/guidance/pupil-premium-information-for-schools-and-alternative-provision-settings [Accessed September 2016].

[13] Gov.uk. (2014). *Pupil premium: funding and accountability for schools – Detailed guidance – GOV.UK.* [online] Available at: https://www.gov.uk/guidance/pupil-premium-information-for-schools-and-alternative-provision-settings [Accessed September 2016].

eligible or have been eligible for free school meals in the last six years and/or looked after children. Schools decide how to spend the funding and need to publish details of how it was spent and the effect it has had on the attainment of those who qualify.

Queensbridge Primary states that Pupil Premium funding is used to implement the most effective educational interventions to address these barriers within the school. Queensbridge Primary uses a needs analysis to identify priority children with the money being spent on specialist teachers, interventions and extracurricular opportunities such as visitors to the school (including the Young Shakespeare Company, Bollywood dancing and Stomp), school trips and after school clubs (including art club, drama club and tap dancing).

Children and the Arts states that *Thousands of children leave school having never set foot in an art gallery, watched a performance in a theatre, or listened to an orchestra play.* The organisation claims that early engagement with the arts has a positive impact by *raising aspirations, increasing confidence, improving communication skills and unlocking creativity.*[14]

> Using a small part of the pupil premium to expand the cultural horizons of less advantaged pupils will prove to be money very well spent indeed.'
>
> Jeremy Newton, Children and the Arts.

This claim identifies why I believed it was important to deliver the Discover Arts Award to Pupil Premium children. The Discover Arts Award is an introductory award for those aged five and above, run by Trinity Collage London. The

---

[14] *Children & the Arts.* [online] Children & the Arts. Available at: http://www.childrenandarts.org.uk/ [Accessed September 2016].

Discover Arts Award would be moderated by myself, a Discover and Explore Assessor.

> To achieve Discover, children and young people discover the arts around them, find out about artists and their work and share their experiences with others, gaining a certificate at the end.
>
> Arts Award, 2016[15]

Therefore I wanted to research the impact of the Discover Arts Award on the confidence of Pupil Premium children and the perceived profile of the arts at Queensbridge based on these children's responses about artists and art forms they have explored.

Background context

The school is a two-form entry inner city school in London with two bulge years which are three form. The school is ethnically and socially diverse with an above average number of children speaking an additional language at home. It has a stable teaching team. The research project was carried out over three forms in Year 2. One teacher was the Art, Design and Literacy Co-ordinator as well as an Arts Award assessor, another teacher was the Speaking and Listening Co-ordinator and prepared children for the Trinity Speech and Drama qualifications during the after school club. The third teacher was an NQT.

The school prides itself on its creative curriculum based on that of Chris Quigley. It is a teaching school and was graded Outstanding in 2011. Arts Mark Gold was achieved in 2014 and the school is hoping to apply for Arts Mark Platinum in 2017. The Executive Head Teacher is an Artsmark critical friend and visits schools as part of them completing the Artsmark award. The school has numerous visitors in

---

[15] *Arts Award Discover – Arts Award.* [online] Artsaward.org.uk. Available at: http://www.artsaward.org.uk/site/?id=2300 [Accessed September 2016].

the arts to the school throughout the year including Bollywood dancing, The Young Shakespeare Company and The Light Theatre. The students take part in numerous art projects such as the whole school calendar project, and trips to the October Gallery and National Gallery. There are numerous after school clubs and children who qualify for Pupil Premium are given priority and one free club per term. Clubs include art club, chess, drama and tap dancing. Children who attend drama club take part in the Trinity Speech and Drama exams in the summer term.

The Story

Arts are used in cross-curricular lessons such as drama and art in History and Literacy lessons however I, along with my Year 2 colleagues, often felt it was challenging to dedicate a prolonged period of time to the arts. After the Year 2 SATs this gave us the opportunity to dedicate two weeks of teaching to completing the Discover Arts Award in the summer term. As a firm believer in an holistic education I believe it is crucial to give children a broad range of opportunities in which to explore their talents. This includes the arts, and by completing the Discover Arts Award, this gave us that opportunity. Our Journeys Topic, which culminated in a trip to the seaside, gave us a wealth of opportunities in which to immerse the children in drama and the visual arts.

How we did it

The Discover Arts Award was completed by all children in Year 2 and this research project focuses on the questionnaire responses of those children who qualified as Pupil Premium.

I initially gave the children in my class questionnaires about their opinions of their lessons and experiences of the arts at Queensbridge. The second half of the summer term allowed us the opportunity to dedicate two weeks to completing the award. The Year 2 Team worked together to plan two weeks of literacy based on *The great Wave Off Kangawa* by Hokusai using drama games about visiting the beach and acting out different seaside scenarios. This culminated in writing a recount, story and personification poem. Over two weeks, afternoon lessons were devoted to experiences in the visual arts. Children did the following: pencil and oil pastel drawings; created marbling images to represent the sea; sculpted shells out of clay; painted using watercolours and poster paints to create sea images based on those by Turner, Lowry and Hokusai; and created reduction prints using polystyrene plates and the school's printing press.

The children's work culminated in a poetry recital to the three classes and a show and tell session to share their artwork with the other children across the year group. The Discover Arts Award was celebrated in a Year 2 assembly with the Head Teacher and Deputy Head Teacher.

Letters were sent home to inform the parents and carers about the project. The children in my class were then given questionnaires after the project about their enjoyment of the arts and their perceived ability in the arts after the project.

Results and impact

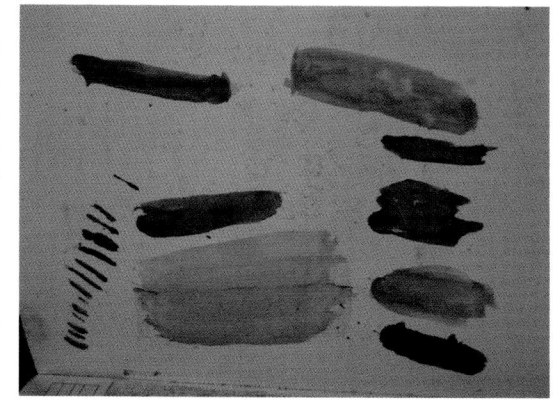

One class completed questionnaires before and after the intervention. Three classes took part in the Discover Arts Award. The initial questionnaire show three out of 12 Pupil Premium children believed they were not good at art compared to one out of 12 after the intervention. Before the intervention four out of 12 Pupil Premium children mentioned that they would like to take part in more arts lessons and believed that these lessons should occur more frequently compared to one child after the intervention. This child commented that taking more lessons would improve their learning about art, drama, music and dance. These results from the questionnaires show a positive impact on all children's self esteem as more children rated themselves as good at the arts after the intervention.

The Questionnaires revealed that after the intervention 12 out of 12 children were positive in their responses to the Arts Award. Children ticked a face to represent how they felt when answering the questions (☺ 😐 ☹). All 12 children selected the happy face for how they felt about the Arts Award. The questions and a sample of answers are shown below.

What did you think of the Discover Arts Award?

'It was fun.' 'I enjoyed it.' 'It was great.' 'I found the arts award good.' 'I think it's good because it helps us learn.'

Did the Discover Arts Award support your learning in visual art and drama?

'Yes!'

What did you enjoy about the Discover Arts Award?

'Painting.' 'I enjoyed marbling.' 'I enjoyed it.' 'I enjoyed the drama.' 'I liked reciting my poem.'

How did you feel about taking part in the Discover Arts Award and achieving your Discover Arts Award?

'It felt great.' 'Proud.' 'Happy.' and 'Good.'

This shows that the Discover Arts Award had a positive impact on the learning of Pupil Premium children (28 out of 28 children were positive about the project).

12 out of 12 Pupil Premium children could name the title of an artwork or famous artist. This was demonstrated in answers to the question 'Which artists and art work did you learn about?' Answers included: Lowry, Hokusai, Turner and *The Great Wave off Kanagawa*. This demonstrates that the

Discover Arts Award raised the profile of the arts in Year 2 for Pupil Premium children.

Observations

Another teacher commented that the Discover Arts Award ensured that all children had the opportunity to explore arts activities. This reveals strengths and talents that may go undiscovered if children do not choose to take up the club opportunities. The teacher gave an example of a Pupil Premium child who is usually quiet in nature. She revealed her speech and drama talents during a poetry recital.

During the planning and delivery of the Discover Arts Award the staff, both the teachers and teaching assistants, were really enthusiastic about the project. Teaching assistants came up with ideas for art lessons and commented on the children's work and progress.

Evaluation

After the intervention all Pupil Premium children were able to identify an artist that they had learnt about. Thereby showing that the Discover Arts Award raised the profile of the arts in their primary education. The Discover Arts Award had a positive impact in raising the children's confidence in the arts. This intervention highlighted the importance of the arts and ensured that this teaching time was safeguarded. By allocating two weeks to complete the Discover Arts Award we can ensure that all children explore a variety of experiences in the arts and celebrate their achievements.

Throughout the research process the Discover Arts Award had a far greater impact than I would ever have imagined. The literacy work that the children produced was outstanding. The poetry recital was really moving and allowed all children to share their talents whether in front of

90 children or their own class. The art work produced was of a brilliant quality and showcased the arts that take place during their education. All children in this study reported that it was a positive experience. Staff were excited and engaged. A teacher highlighted that by explicitly planning for drama they strengthened their pedagogy and allowed subjects that have been sidelined to take prominence.

Next steps

The next steps for this project are to share the impact with the rest of the school to highlight the importance of the arts and how the Discover Arts Award benefits all children, including those who qualify as Pupil Premium, by giving them opportunities to discover talents in the arts and celebrate their success. I will ensure that the Discover Arts Award becomes an embedded practice in Year 2 to celebrate the breadth of the curriculum at Queensbridge school. As the Art and Design Co-ordinator in a teaching school, I have recently set up an Arts Forum with other schools in the alliance. I will be sharing this research project with the other Art Co-ordinators across the other schools. I will be highlighting the benefits to children's self esteem and knowledge of the arts, which is especially important for Pupil Premium children who may not get these experiences or much exposure to the arts outside of school. Giving children access to the Discover Arts Award ensures that time is given to the arts as well as highlighting the importance of the arts in the curriculum. I found that the Discover Arts Award allowed us to further celebrate children's achievements in the arts as a school. At Queensbridge, we are always celebrating children's achievements in the arts in Star Assemblies, the school website and Twitter. The Discover Arts Award allowed us to further celebrate every child's achievements and gave the teaching staff an opportunity to discover children's hidden talents which can be further developed and fostered.

I would recommend completing the Discover Arts Award to other schools, as Pupil Premium children were found to gain confidence in the arts and developed their knowledge and understanding of the arts and artists. The current study benefitted from staff members already feeling confident in teaching visual art and drama and therefore being able to plan a scheme of work independently. So the results of this study could be transferred to other settings if staff were given the freedom in how they delivered the award and teacher skill sets were shared across the staff. In this current study the Arts Award was taught in areas of the arts that the teachers enjoyed and at least one member of staff felt confident in teaching. Teaching skills in the visual arts and drama were shared between the three teachers.

Limitations of this study include children answering the questions knowing that I would be looking at them and therefore giving answers that would please me. Again, staff already know about my enthusiasm for the arts and this may have influenced the study.

References

Arts Award, 2016 Available at:
http://www.artsaward.org.uk/site/?id=2300 [Accessed August 2016].
Children and the Arts, 2016 Available at:
http://www.childrenandarts.org.uk/about-us/ [Accessed August 2016].
Department for Education 2016 Available at:
https://www.gov.uk/guidance/pupil-premium-information-for-schools-and-alternative-provision-settings [Accessed August 2016].
Queensbridge Primary School Available at:
http://www.queensbridge.hackney.sch.uk/our-school/school-policies/pupil-premium-2/ [Accessed August 2016].

Acknowledgements

The Editors would like to thank:

All of the Cultural Leaders and their schools.

All who support cultural and arts education in London.

Alice Edwards, Laura Fuller and the rest of the fabulous A New Direction team.

Andy Buck, Leadership Matters.

Anja Teichert, Danielle Wood and Matt Overd, NotDeadFish.

David Woods CBE, London Leadership Strategy.

Hannah Wilmot, Evaluator.

Jan Polack, University of the First Age.

John Kelleher, Teacher and Musician.

Kevin Grist, Musical Futures.

Cover design by Spiffing Covers
Typesetting by Hope Services
Printing by Rapidity
Produced by A New Direction & NotDeadFish
Published by NotDeadFish Publishing